You Ca

This book is dedicated to my darling wife.
Thank you for all your love. Truly you have
been a wonderful helpmate. I love you.

You Can Fly

Andy Economides

Silver Fish
publishing

Omnibus edition published in Great Britain 1998 by
Silver Fish Publishing.

British Library Cataloguing in Publication Data
A record for this book is available from the British Library

ISBN 1 902134 07 9

Printed and bound in Great Britain by
Cox & Wyman, Reading, Berks.

Silver Fish Publishing is a division of
Silver Fish Creative Marketing Ltd
44c Fermoy Road, Maida Vale
London W9 3NH

Contents

Acknowledgements

A big heartfelt thank you to J. John for many years of amazing friendship, fun and input.

To my mother Cleo - thank you so much for your love and for the sacrifices you have made. I love you.

A special thank you to the friends, partners and supporters of Soteria Trust who enable us to share the good news of Jesus in Britain and other countries.

Thank you to my wife - without you this book would not have been created.

Last but not least, lots of love to my daughter Hannah for just being you and for the joy that you bring.

Foreword

It gives me great pleasure to write a foreword to Andy Economides' book *You Can Fly*. Andy bounced into my life in the Autumn of 1974 when we were both students in London. His enthusiasm was contagious - the word enthusiasm comes from the Greek word *En Theos* - which means 'in God'. Andy was certainly in God! Andy built a bridge from him to me and when he did Christ Jesus walked over it. Andy also continued to disciple me in the Christian faith and pushed me out of my comfort zones to validate my Christian faith in thought, word and deed. Andy was a good mentor because he modelled what he taught.

You Can Fly has 26 chapters, each commencing with one of the letters of the alphabet. It is a literary bouquet - you choose your flower and wear it that day. If it turns out to be a cactus I am sure Andy did mean well.

No one book can do it all, but suppose you could spend the day with Andy Economides talking; what would you talk about? - Jesus, change, temptation, perseverance, faith, gifts, healing, love, relationships, vision, difficulties in the Christian life. This is what this book is about.

You Can Fly:

is challenging and comforting
is instructive and inspiring
is poignant and practical
is refreshing and relevant

Andy is best known for his uncompromising and straightforward message of the power of God and the practical outworkings of his presence in our lives today.

If you have just become a Christian, may this book be like a 'starter pack' in laying some foundations to build on as you live out the Christian life. If you have been a Christian for a while you will find this book a refreshing tonic and I trust you will find this book inspires your faith as a sound sense for living - which is what happened to me when I read it!

Christians, like pianos, need frequent tuning - this book will do it.

J. John

Chapter 1

Abuse

There are many different kinds of abuse: physical, emotional, sexual, verbal and spiritual. All abuse is wrong and sinful. The word abuse can mean: to use for a bad purpose, use to bad effect, maltreat, use incorrectly or improperly, insult verbally, to use unjust or corrupt language, or to misuse.

Abuse does enormous harm to its victims. Child sexual abuse is an abuse of adult power. Children who have suffered sexual abuse are deeply hurt. Many have their lives ruined with scars that never heal.

Today more and more individuals are suffering non-physical abuse from their employers. They are being recognised as victims of abuse and are compensated through the courts.

For men, women and children who have suffered physical or sexual abuse, there are organisations and groups who offer help and understanding. (Please see the sources of help for physical and sexual abuse victims, at the back of the book.)

There is also another kind of abuse - spiritual. It is regrettable that some Christians do not believe that spiritual abuse exists. Perhaps those that hold such a view have not suffered in this way or are abusers themselves. Some do not or will not understand the problem of spiritual abuse. Others belittle it and think that it is not a serious matter. In some cases those that have suffered spiritual abuse can be as damaged or hurt as much as those who have suffered other forms of abuse.

What is Spiritual Abuse?

In their book *The Subtle Power of Spiritual Abuse*, on the subject of recognising and escaping spiritual manipulation and false spiritual authority within the Church, authors David Johnson and Jeff VanVonderen write:

> Spiritual abuse is the mistreatment of a person who is in need of help, support or greater spiritual empowerment, with the weakening, undermining or decreasing that person's spiritual empowerment.
>
> It often involves overriding the feelings and opinions of others, without regard to what will result in the other person's state of living, emotions or spiritual well-being. [1]

Overriding the feelings of others is a characteristic of those who abuse others. The abusers do not mind or care that they are overriding the victims, so long as they get what they want or need for themselves.

Marc Dupont in *Walking Out of Spiritual Abuse* defines abuse as follows:

> Abuse is the misuse of power. Whether the abuse is emotional, physical, sexual, or spiritual, it is always about the wrongful use of power and authority. Power used by an individual to control, manipulate, and/or use another. The end result for the victim is damage. It may be physical harm, emotional harm, sexual harm, spiritual harm, or a combination of those. Abuse is always about those with power or authority using their power or authority wrongfully in order to compensate for their fears, hurts, and insecurities. [2]

Those in positions of power and authority need to be very careful about themselves; they need to be careful about wrong desires, especially the desires to dominate. A desire to control and dominate others can arise from a poor and insecure self image. Those who are insecure in themselves or their job will tend to dominate others. They get their measure of satisfaction from knowing they can control others. This desire to control and manipulate comes from pride, not humility. Such people must recognise and respect that each individual has an opinion. Manipulators and controllers cannot, will not, accept differences of opinion. A leader's fear of failure can cause a desire to dominate.

Nigerian evangelist and author, Prince Yinka Oyekan Junior writes:

> To dominate or lord it over another person is therefore an attempt to extend one's sphere of domination over and against what God originally intended. [3]

Are You Safe?

There is no such thing as a perfect church or family. People get hurt wherever they are. However there are people, groups and churches that are abusive and there are those that are not. Abusive churches are not healthy places. Abusive churches are not safe places.

In the nature of my work I visit many people and places. It is sad that there are individuals in leadership positions of churches that abuse the very people they are supposed to be caring for. Some people, some churches are not safe. David Johnson and Jeff VanVonderen have written:

> The difference between an abusive and non-abusive system is that while hurtful behaviours might happen in both, it is not permissible to talk about the problems, hurts and abuses in the abusive system. Hence there is no healing and restoration after the wound has occurred, and the victim is made to feel at fault for questioning or pointing out the problem. [4]

In a spiritually abusive system, if you have spoken out concerning abusive behaviour, you have got in trouble, although you are innocent. You have become a problem by speaking out. Whether you speak for yourself or on behalf of others there will be a price to pay. People need wisdom to know how, when and where it is time to act.

There is too much indifference and apathy in the Church and in the world. Christ was not indifferent. He cared about those who were abused. He spoke up for them. He went to them and comforted them.

I have a friend who is being battered by the words and actions of the minister of his church. Will anyone stand with him? Will someone do something useful and practical?

Elie Wiesel was a holocaust survivor and is an international advocate for its survivors. In Germany, he delivered a famous speech before former President of the United States, Ronald Reagan. He said:

> I have learned of the danger of indifference, the crime of indifference. For the opposite of love, I have learned is not hate, but indifference. Jews were killed by the enemy but betrayed by their so-called allies, who found political reasons to justify their indifference or passivity. What have I learned? When there is obvious injustice and principles are violated - when human lives and dignity are at stake - when your allies find reasons to justify their silence or indifference - neutrality is a sin. [5]

Indifference matters to others. It can cost them dearly if no one shows practical love and care. Indifference or neutrality is a sin against God and others. Indifference in the Church can create damage and hurt. It is the sin of omission. It is as serious as adultery or stealing.

Jesus brought freedom and liberty in His teaching and by His actions. The message of Jesus is one of joy and freedom. Jesus said:

> *'Then you will know the truth, and the truth will set you free. So if the Son sets you free, you will be free indeed.'*
> (John 8:32,36)

In abusive churches there is a lack of freedom taught from the front. In abusive churches the congregation is being kept back from joy and freedom; there is doom and gloom. You can sense the darkness. To the undiscerning or unknowing, everything seems fine. Spiritually abusive systems or churches are unhappy. They should carry a health warning: 'Being in this church can damage your health'.

Paul enjoyed freedom, not to do whatever he pleased, but a freedom that brought health, life and blessing to those he ministered to. Paul encouraged the Christians:

> *It is for freedom that Christ has set us free. Stand firm, then, and do not let yourselves be burdened again by a yoke of slavery* (Galatians 5:1).

To the Christians at the church in Corinth, he warned,

> *You were bought at a price; do not become slaves of men* (1 Corinthians 7:23).

Are you suffering from spiritual abuse? If you are you will know it. Help yourself. Do not allow a church, group or an individual to dominate, control or intimidate you. Walk away. Walk out of spiritual abuse. Enjoy your freedom in Christ. One of the difficulties for those who have been abused is to be able to trust again. This is understandable. It is possible to slowly make a recovery and to be able to trust others. This does take time. You have good reason to be cautious.

There are those who dominate and control who say, 'You can trust me'. Trust is not something that can be demanded. Trust is gained or lost on the basis of integrity and honesty. I do not trust all Christians. Some lie and some are dishonest. There are spiritual leaders who lead a double life. Jesus warned us about them:

> *'So you must obey them and do everything they tell you. But do not do what they do, for they do not practise what they preach.'* (Matthew 23:3)

Double talk is another characteristic of someone who does not have integrity. Often they will not say what they mean and at other times not mean what they say. Those who practise double talk lie to look good, to get what they want, to get out of trouble. Things they say have a double meaning. It is difficult to know where you stand with these people. They are slippery people. These people can wear you down so much, you despair.

How to Spot an Abusive Church

Those who abuse cause damage and hurt to their victims. If we can recognise the signs or characteristics of a spiritually abusive church or system we can avoid getting hurt.

Marc Dupont lists eight classic warning signs that are common in spiritually abusive churches or systems: [6]

1.　Prevailing attitudes of elitism and/or isolation
2.　Leaders practising 'cursing' or judging
3.　Denial of freewill and invasion of privacy
4.　Leadership without accountability
5.　Hazy boundaries between serving God and leaders
6.　Legalism and condemnation
7.　Scapegoating and denial syndromes
8.　A continuous turnover of leaders and staff

Speaking of leadership, including pastors within the church, Dr D. Hocking has this to say:

> If you cannot submit to authority yourself, you cannot expect others to submit to you. [7]

The one who is the overall leader of the church, whether priest, pastor, minister or clergyman, must be accountable to others within the church, an accountability that actually works. In theory the pastor may be accountable, but in practice it does not always work out. Some pastors do what they want to anyway, whether it is right or wrong. When the pastor is not submitting to authority, things can and do go wrong. People in the congregation can get seriously hurt. It is an absurd belief that those at the top are accountable only to God.

A friend told me that in his church his pastor has told the other elders, and the church, that the elders are accountable to him and that he is accountable only to God. Very convenient and very unbiblical. This is dangerous.

It is a safeguard for pastors to be accountable in practice. It is a safeguard for others as well as for themselves. This requires

Chapter 3
Cross of Christ

A Day That Changed Her World

My mother Cleo and my father Demetrakis came to England to start a new life. They lived in Britain for many years working and raising their children. In May 1997 they finally accomplished the one thing that was close to their hearts. They returned to their homeland of Cyprus to retire. Both had worked very hard throughout their working lives. For many years they had longed and waited for this day. I felt so pleased for them. At last they would enjoy peace on this beautiful island.

Although home was small, it was comfortable and provided all they needed. Unknown to Cleo something was to happen that would change the rest of her life and even the lives of others. For Cleo it would be a shocking and dreadful event. The Tuesday of that week my parents arrived in Cyprus. For the next two days they began to settle down to their new life. During those days they unpacked cases and cleaned through their home. They visited relatives and friends. On Thursday my father was on the balcony of their flat when terror struck. Suddenly he had heart and breathing problems. He called for help. My mother came to him. She called for help. In a short space of time he died.

At the age of 64, having at last returned, to his country of origin, to retire in peace - it was too late. My mother witnessed the death of the man she had loved and lived with for many years. It was the day that changed her world. Her life will never be the same again.

People all over the world face events, as a result of which their world changes. These changes can be for better or for worse.

That Was Something Else

Two thousand years ago something wonderful happened that

would affect the world for ever. It was the day that changed the world. Indeed the day that changed history. It was the day God's son, Jesus Christ, died. Today the Church celebrates that day on what is called, 'Good Friday'. The only reason that it was a 'good' Friday was that three days later Jesus rose from the dead. Today the Church calls that special Sunday Easter Day.

Jesus voluntarily gave up his life for a reason. We begin our examination of the events that took place starting at the garden in Gethsemane. Gethsemane was on the lower slopes of the Mount of Olives, just outside Jerusalem, one of Jesus' favourite places.

Gethsemane

> *Then they arrived at a place called Gethsemane, and Jesus said to his disciples, 'Sit down here while I pray.' He took with him Peter, James and John, and began to be horror-stricken and desperately depressed. 'My heart is nearly breaking,' he told them. 'Stay here and keep watch for me.' Then he walked forward a little way and flung himself on the ground, praying that, if it were possible, he might not have to face the ordeal. 'Dear Father,' he said 'all things are possible to you. Please- let me not have to drink this cup! Yet it is not what I want but what you want.'*
>
> *Then he came and found them fast asleep. He spoke to Peter, 'Are you asleep, Simon? Couldn't you manage to watch for a single hour? Watch and pray, all of you, that you may not have to face temptation. Your spirit is willing, but human nature is weak.'*
>
> *Then he went away again and prayed in the same words, and once more he came and found them asleep. They could not keep their eyes open and they did not know what to say for themselves. When he came back a third time, he said, 'Are you still going to sleep and take your ease? All right - the moment has come; now you are going to see the Son of Man betrayed into the hands of evil men! Get up, let us be going! Look, here comes my betrayer!'* (Mark 14:32-42. J. B. Phillips)

Jesus expressed to his dear friends, who had been with him from the beginning, his deep distress and troubled heart. His heart was overwhelmed with sorrow, almost to the point of death. He asked help from his disciples. He needed their friendship, now more than ever. *'Stay here and keep watch,'* Jesus asks them. Moving away from Peter, James and John he falls to the ground. He cannot help it. He knows the abuse, suffering, and evil that was to come. Jesus prays to his heavenly Father, asking that if possible God might take the cup of suffering away from him. But he would rather do God's will whatever the cost and therefore acknowledges that he will drink the deadly cup. While Jesus is talking to his sleepy disciples, Judas the betrayer approaches, bringing others with him, to arrest Jesus.

Jesus Arrested

Just as he was speaking, Judas, one of the Twelve, appeared. With him was a crowd armed with swords and clubs, sent from the chief priests, the teachers of the law, and the elders.

Now the betrayer had arranged a signal with them: 'The one I kiss is the man; arrest him and lead him away under guard.' Going at once to Jesus, Judas said, 'Rabbi!' and kissed him. The men seized Jesus and arrested him. Then one of those standing near drew his sword and struck the servant of the high priest, cutting off his ear. 'Am I leading a rebellion,' said Jesus, 'that you have come out with swords and clubs to capture me? Every day I was with you, teaching in the temple courts, and you did not arrest me. But the Scriptures must be fulfilled.'
Then everyone deserted him and fled (Mark 14:43-50).

Judas was aware that people knew Jesus well enough by sight. He felt that in the dim light of the garden, that they needed a definite indication who they were to arrest. He chose the most terrible of signs - a kiss. It was customary to greet a rabbi with a kiss. It was a sign of respect, affection for a well-loved teacher. There is a dreadful thing here, when Judas says, *'The one I kiss is the man.'* He uses the word *philein*, which is the ordinary word for kiss. When it is written that he kissed Jesus, the word used is *kata philein*. The *kata*, is intensive. Kata philein means to kiss as a lover kisses his beloved. The sign of betrayal was not a mere form of kiss of respectful greeting. It was a lover's kiss. That is the most grim and awful thing in all the gospel story.

The arresting mob came from the chief priests, the scribes and the elders, the three sections of the Sanhedrin police, the Jewish religious council. They marched Jesus away to the high priest. The disciples' nerves cracked. They could not face it. They were afraid that they too would share the fate prepared for Jesus. They all left him and fled. Through all this, Jesus displays serenity, for the struggle in the garden was over. Now there was the peace of a man who knows that he is following the will of God.

Jesus Before the High Priest

They took Jesus to the high priest, and all the chief priests, elders and teachers of the law came together. Peter followed him at a distance, right into the courtyard of the high priest. There he sat with the guards and warmed himself at the fire.

The chief priests and the whole Sanhedrin were looking for evidence against Jesus so that they could put him to death, but they did not find any. Many testified falsely against him, but their statements did not agree.

Then some stood up and gave this false testimony against him: 'We heard him say, "I will destroy this man made temple and in three days will build another, not made by man".' Yet even their testimony did not agree.

Then the high priest stood up before them and asked Jesus, 'Are you not going to answer? What is this testimony that these men are bringing against you?' But Jesus remained silent and gave no answer.

Again the high priest asked him, 'Are you the Christ, the son of the Blessed One?'

'I am,' said Jesus. 'And you will see the Son of Man sit-

*ting at the right hand of the Mighty One and coming on
the clouds of heaven.'*

*The high priest tore his clothes. 'Why do we need any
more witnesses?' he asked. 'You have heard the blasphe-
my. What do you think?'*

*They all condemned him as worthy of death. Then
some began to spit at him; they blindfolded him, struck
him with their fists, and said, 'Prophesy!' And the guards
took him and beat him* (Mark 14:53-65).

This religious trial was grossly unfair and unlawful. Many
testified falsely against him, but their statements did not agree.

The high priest was exasperated. He asked the question which
he knew would get the result he wanted - a verdict of death.
'Are you the Christ, the son of the Blessed One?' Jesus
answered *'I am.'* That was it. They condemned him worthy of
death. The issue here was not about any unlawful deed that
Jesus may have done. Jesus never did anything that was unlawful or sinful. They sentenced him to death because of who he
claimed to be. He claimed to be the Son of God and the
Messiah.

Having passed sentence, they began to spit at him, they blindfolded him and hit him with their fists, taunting him saying,
'Guess who hit you?' The guards took him and beat him.

Very early the next morning the chief priests, with the elders,
the teachers of the law and the whole Sanhedrin reached a decision. They bound Jesus, led him away and handed him over to
Pilate. He was to be tried under the state now.

Jesus Before Pilate

Pilate wanted to release Jesus, because he knew that it was out
of envy that the chief priests had handed Jesus over to him. The
continued pressure from the religious leaders and the crowd
finally weakened Pilate's resolve to free Jesus. He changed his
mind. Now he wanted to satisfy the crowd. He ordered Jesus to
be flogged and then crucified.

Roman flogging was a terrible thing. The criminal was taken

to a post and stripped naked. The scourge was a long leathery thong, studded here and there with sharpened bits of lead and bone. It literally tore a man's back to ribbons. Sometimes it tore out a man's eye. Some men died under it. Some men emerged from the ordeal raving mad. Few retained consciousness throughout. This is what they inflicted on Jesus. The flogging completed. The soldiers begin to mock Jesus.

> *The soldiers led Jesus away into the palace (that is the Praetorium) and called together the whole company of soldiers. They put a purple robe on him, then twisted together a crown of thorns and set it on him. And they began to call out to him, 'Hail, King of the Jews!' Again and again they struck him on the head with a staff and spit on him. Falling on their knees, they paid homage to him. And when they had mocked him, they took off the purple robe and put his own clothes on him. Then they led him out to crucify him* (Mark 15:16-20).

William Barclay describes what happened the day that Jesus allowed himself to be crucified:

The routine of the crucifixion did not alter. When the cross was prepared the criminal had himself to carry it to the place of execution. He was placed in the middle of a hollow square of four soldiers. In front marched a soldier carrying a board stating the crime of which the prisoner was guilty. The board was afterwards affixed to the cross. They took not the shortest but the longest way to the place of execution. They followed every possible street and lane so that as many as possible should see and take warning. When they reached the place of crucifixion, the cross was laid flat on the ground. The prisoner was stretched upon it and his hands nailed to it. The feet were not nailed but only loosely bound. Between the prisoner's legs projected a ledge of wood called a saddle, to take his weight when the cross was raised upright - otherwise the nails would have torn through the flesh of the hands. The cross was then lifted upright and set in its socket - and the criminal was left to die. The cross was not tall. It was shaped like the letter T, and had no top piece at all. Sometimes prisoners hung for as long as a week, slowly dying of hunger and of thirst, suffering sometimes to the point of actual madness.

They offered Jesus drugged wine and he would not drink it. A company of pious and merciful women in Jerusalem came to every crucifixion and gave the criminals a drink of drugged wine to ease the terrible pain. They offered this to Jesus - and he refused it.

Jesus was resolved to taste death at its bitterest and to go to God with open eyes.

The soldiers diced for his clothes. We have seen how the prisoner was marched to the place of crucifixion amid four soldiers. These soldiers had as their perquisite the clothes of the criminal. Now a Jew wore five articles of clothing - the inner robe, the outer robe, the sandals, the girdle and the turban. When the four lesser things had been assigned, that left the great outer robe. It would have been useless to cut it up, and so the soldiers gambled for it in the shadow of the Cross.

Jesus was crucified between two thieves. It was a symbol of his whole life that even at the end he companied with sinners. [1]

Boundless Love

Jesus suffered much abuse but it was not over yet. Let Mark tell us in his words.

It was the third hour when they crucified him. The written notice of the charge against him read: THE KING OF THE JEWS. They crucified two robbers with him, one on his right and one on his left. Those who passed by hurled insults at him, shaking their heads and saying, 'So! You who are going to destroy the temple and build it three days, come down from the cross and save yourself!'

In the same way the chief priests and the teachers of the law mocked him among themselves. 'He saved others,' they said, but he can't save himself! Let this Christ, this King of Israel, come down now from the cross, that we may see and believe.'

Those crucified with him also heaped insults on him.

At the sixth hour darkness came over the whole land until the ninth hour. And at the ninth hour Jesus cried out in a loud voice, 'Eloi, Eloi, lama sabachthani?' - which means 'My God, my God, why have you forsaken me?'

When some of those standing near heard this, they said, 'Listen, he's calling Elijah.'

One man ran, filled a sponge with wine vinegar, put it on a stick, and offered it to Jesus to drink. 'Now leave him alone. Let's see if Elijah comes to take him down,' he said.

With a loud cry, breathed his last.

The curtain of the temple was torn in two from top to bottom. And when a centurion, who stood there in front of Jesus, heard his cry and saw how he died, he said, 'Surely this man was the Son of God!' (Mark 15:25-39).

As evening approached Joseph of Arimathea, a prominent member of the council, went to Pilate and asked for Jesus' body. Pilate, having received confirmation of Jesus' death, gave permission for Joseph to take the body.

Joseph had Jesus' body wrapped in linen and placed in a tomb cut out of rock. A stone was rolled against the entrance of the tomb.

The Empty Tomb

Early on the first day of the week, while it was still dark, Mary Magdalene went to the tomb and saw that the stone had been removed from the entrance. So she came running to Simon Peter and the other disciple, the one Jesus loved, and said, 'They have taken the Lord out of the tomb, and we don't know where they have put him.'

So Peter and the other disciple started for the tomb. Both were running, but the other disciple outran Peter and reached the tomb first. He bent over and looked in at the strips of linen lying there but did not go in. Then Simon Peter, who was behind him, arrived and went into the tomb. He saw the strips of linen lying there, as well as the burial cloth that had been around Jesus' head. The cloth was folded up by itself, separate from the linen. Finally the other disciple, who reached the tomb first, also went inside. He saw and believed (John 20:1-8).

One thing is certain - if Jesus had not risen from the dead, we would never of heard of him. The attitude of the women was that they had come to pay their last tribute to a dead man. The attitude of the disciples was that everything had finished in tragedy. By far the best proof of the resurrection is the existence of the Christian Church. Nothing else could have changed sad and despairing men and women into people radiant with joy and flaming with courage. The resurrection is the central fact of the whole Christian faith.

Because we believe in the resurrection something important follows. Jesus is a living presence not just a person in a book. It is not enough to study the story of Jesus. We may begin that way but we move on to meeting Him. The Christian life is not the life of a person who *knows about* Jesus, but the life of a person who *knows* Jesus. There is all the difference in the world between knowing about a person and knowing a person. Most people know about Queen Elizabeth or the President of the United States of America, but not so many actually know them.

Knowing Jesus means knowing life to the full. Know Jesus - know life. No Jesus - no life.

Know Jesus - Know Life

Jesus Christ gave up his life willingly. He allowed his life to be taken. He was in control, although the people responsible for his death thought that they were.

While Jesus hung on the cross he cried out those incredible words, 'It is finished!' He immediately breathed his last, gave up his spirit and died. It was a cry of victory: 'I have done it!' He accomplished his ultimate purpose for visiting our world, that of dying and shedding his blood for our sin and shame. The blood of Jesus brings forgiveness.

Jesus' disciple Peter writing in his epistle concerning the cross of Jesus says, *'For Christ died for sins once for all, the righteous for the unrighteous, to bring you to God.'* (1 Peter 3:18)

It was for sins that Christ died. The good and righteous one died for us so that we could come to God. Our being brought to God means living in close friendship with God, knowing him and meeting him. That is eternal life. It is knowing God and Jesus Christ, not knowing about but actually knowing God and his Son Jesus (John 17:3).

The prophet Isaiah prophesied about the coming Messiah or Christ:

> *He was pierced for our transgressions, he was crushed for our iniquities; the punishment that bought us peace was upon him, and by his wounds we are healed. We all, like sheep, have gone astray, each of us has turned to his own way; and the Lord has laid on him the iniquity of us all* (Isaiah 53:5-6).

On the cross Jesus literally took our transgressions on himself. Transgressions means breaking God's laws. We have all done that. He carried our iniquity. Iniquity is the evil that we have done. He was punished that we may have peace. Peace with God. Peace with ourselves.

You can know God and Jesus. You can know forgiveness. You can experience becoming a new creation. All of this is done by God. It is his power coming within your life and transforming your life. It is being born again by the Holy Spirit. For this to happen, you need to do your part. Receive and believe Jesus Christ the Son of God.

> *Some however did receive him and believed in him so he gave them the right to become God's children. They did not become God's children by natural means that is by*

being born as the children of a human father, God him-self was their father (John 1:12-13).

Receive and Believe

Receiving Jesus means to welcome him into your life. He wants to come and live within your life by his Spirit. Jesus stands at the door of your life and knocks, waiting for you to open the door and invite him in. He says:

> 'Here I am! I stand at the door and knock. If anyone hears my voice and opens the door, I will come in and eat with him and he with me.' (Revelation 3:20)

To receive Jesus means to no longer live your life without him. It involves receiving his ways and purposes for our lives.

The second thing you need to do is believe that God so loved the world he gave his only son to be crucified for your sins. It means believing in God's risen son Jesus. Believing is trusting. Will you put your trust in the Cross of Christ? Put your trust and life in his life. For those that believe and receive, a miracle happens - they become God's children by experiencing the new birth.

Think of Jesus knocking now, asking to come into your life. You want him to come into your life or perhaps you want to make sure he has come into your life. It may help you to say this prayer quietly, phrase by phrase, thinking carefully what you are saying, what you are doing.

Lord Jesus Christ, I have sinned in my thoughts,
words and actions.
There are many good things I have not done.
There are many sinful things I have done.
I am sorry for my sins and turn from everything
I know to be wrong.
You gave your life on the cross for me.
Gratefully I give my life to you.
I ask you to come into my life by your Holy

Spirit.
Come in as my Saviour to cleanse me.
Come in as my friend and be with me.
I will serve you all the remaining years of my
life. Amen.

Asking Jesus into your life is just the first step - like shaking hands with someone you have just met. Getting to know someone well takes time and effort. It is the same with Jesus. We can get to know Jesus better through the Bible, through prayer and through the local church. Most importantly God has given you the Holy Spirit to enable and empower you. The Holy Spirit is a wonderful person available to you, to help you become like Jesus. The Holy Spirit will comfort, strengthen and guide you. Please turn to the chapter on the Holy Spirit for further help.

Chapter 4
Don't Get On The Roof

The shepherd boy became king. He restored peace and great military power to the nation of Israel. David achieved personal greatness and popularity. He showed justice, mercy and fairness to enemies, rebels, allies and friends. His reign came from his faith in God. He regarded God's interest as more important than his own until one Spring evening.

David sent Joab with his officers and the Israelite army out to war at the time of year when kings usually go to war. David stayed in Jerusalem. Unknown to him it was the beginning of a series of tragic events brought on by himself. He was led from triumph to trouble because of his passion for prosperity and ease.

Falling Deeper and Deeper

David abandoned his responsibility as leader and king by remaining at home from battle. He was in the wrong place. He had committed a serious mistake (2 Samuel 2).

One evening David got up from his bed and went to the palace roof. As he walked about up there, his eyes saw a very beautiful woman. His eyes and mind begin to focus on his own desires. Martin Luther said, 'Sin is essentially a departure from God.'[1] David sends someone to find out who the woman is. Instead of turning away from temptation he looked into it. It was wrong of David to have gone this far. As St. Augustine said, 'Sin is energy in the wrong channel'. [2]

'It is Bathsheba, the wife of Uriah' reports the messenger. Others are sent to fetch her. David sleeps with Bathsheba. He commits adultery.

A person is tempted when they drawn away and trapped by their own evil desire. Then their evil desire conceives and gives birth to sin. Sin when it is fully grown brings death (James 1:14-15).

David brought temptation upon himself. Then he deliberately sinned. We must not think of mistakes, most made unintentionally, as sin. Neither must we think of sin the way we do mistakes. David's first fatal mistake was to be on the roof instead of at war. The subsequent event with Bathsheba was unlawful and sinful.

Later Bathsheba discovered that she was pregnant and sent a message to inform David of the fact. David sent for Uriah, her husband, under the pretence of seeking information about the course of the war. His intention was to cover up his sin by deceiving others. He instructs Uriah to go home and rest a while. David is desperately hoping that Uriah will sleep with Bathsheba, so that the baby could be seen to be his. Uriah does not go home as he believes it is his duty to be with his men, in order to continue to offer them support.

David tries a different approach. This time he gets Uriah drunk in the hope that he will then go home and sleep with Bathsheba. Uriah remained in the guard room and did not return home.

David allowed himself to fall deeper and deeper into sin. He ordered Joab, the commander of the army, to put Uriah in the front line of the battle where the fighting was heaviest, then to retreat allowing him to be killed. This is exactly what happened. In addition some of David's innocent officers were killed. David committed murder to continue the cover-up. Sins are like ripples in water. When a stone is thrown into a pool of water, one ripple produces another.

Bathsheba mourned the death of her husband. David sent for her when her time of mourning was over and she became his wife and bore him a son. God was not pleased with what David had done (2 Samuel 11:26-27).

At any time David could have stopped his evil actions, but it is difficult to stop once sin starts. The deeper the mess, the less people want to admit having done wrong. It is much easier to stop sliding down a hill when you are near the top than when you are half-way down. There is a better way for all concerned. The best solution is to stop before it starts.

The Consequences of David's Sin Affected Many Others

Covering up his deeds and lies lasted for only so long. Your sins will find you out. Eventually David, the King of all Israel, had his sin exposed. In response to the prophetic ministry of Nathan he confessed his sin, repented and was assured of forgiveness:

> Then David said to Nathan, 'I have sinned against the Lord.' Nathan replied, 'The Lord has taken away your sin. You are not going to die. But because by doing this you have made the enemies of the Lord show utter contempt, the son born to you will die.' (2 Samuel 12:13-14)

The prophet told what will happen to David and those around him:

> Now, therefore, the sword shall never depart from your house, because you despised me and took the wife of Uriah the Hittite to be your own. This is what the Lord says: 'Out of your own household I am going to bring calamity upon you. Before your very eyes I will take your wives and give them to one who is close to you, and he will lie with your wives in broad daylight. You did it in secret, but I will do this thing in broad daylight before all Israel.' (2 Samuel 12:10-12)

The word of the Lord was fulfilled. Absalom, one of David's sons, killed his brother Amnon (2 Samuel 13:26-30). Absalom himself was later killed (2 Samuel 18:14-15). Secondly, Absalom rebels against his father and turns many Israelites' loyalty away from David towards himself (2 Samuel 15:13). David's wives were given to Absalom to have sex with in public view (2 Samuel 16:20-22).

The consequences of David's sin were irreversible. Sometimes an apology is not enough. When God forgives us and restores our relationship with him, he does not eliminate all of the consequences of our wrongdoing. We may be tempted to say, 'If this is wrong, I can always apologise to God.' We must remember that we may set into motion events with irreversible consequences.

Better to be Safe Than Sorry

Recently we called the gas inspector to our home to check for a leak, as we had smelt gas within the house. It caused a slight inconvenience but it was better to be safe than sorry. No escape of gas could be detected from the fire, boiler or mains. We could not take any chances with gas exploding, causing fire and damage to ourselves and our neighbours.

In life it is vital to take safety measures to prevent danger or harm. Some people may see safety measures as inconvenient or unnecessary. There is no price to high to pay for safety, certainty and enjoyment with God and others. In every aspect of our lives, especially in our relationships and dealings with others, we must be careful or we could fall.

The early part of David's life was full of music and dancing. The latter part held mourning and lamentation. It was this scandal that divided David's life into contrasting parts.

I do not believe that he should have been on the roof in the first place. What followed could have been avoided. The result was tragic. The rest of his life was ruined even though forgiveness was granted.

The three common sins are in the areas of pride, money and sexual misbehaviour. There are five steps we can take to help us avoid sin and destructive behaviour:

1 Don't get on the roof. Instead, go on to fulfil your true purpose.

2 Set a guard. Nehemiah was practical and prayerful against possible destruction. *'They plotted together to come and fight against Jerusalem and stir up trouble against it. But we prayed to our God and posted a guard day and night to meet this threat.'* (Nehemiah 4:8-9)

3 Flee temptation (2 Timothy 2:22). Do not look at it or entertain it. Run - it is the only thing to do. Do not be naive about your capacity to sin, however strong you think you are.

4 Pray. Prayer is important, but on its own, it is not enough. Pray that you will not be led into temptation.

5 Learn from David and Bathsheba. The day to day choices that we make are very important. Have you asked for God's help with today's decisions? Especially those decisions where you may be vulnerable?

Mary Pytches in her excellent book *Between Friends* writes:

> The Bible says we should be *'as shrewd as snakes and as innocent as doves'*. I think this means we must be wise about temptation and the attractions of evil, but that we should be innocent in our experience of sin. We are wise and will remain innocent when we 'stay always within the boundaries where God's love can reach and bless us'. [3]

Mary then sets out some extremely helpful safety measures that can enhance our lives, if put into practice. This is what she writes:

1 Firstly, pray that God will indicate the appropriate boundaries for each new relationship.

2 Secondly, we must think ahead to the consequences of stepping outside these boundaries. Never be afraid to face the possible damage and destruction which could be wrought should lines be crossed.

I remember many years ago now taking a ride in a car with a fellow missionary. He had recently, like me, experienced a new release of the Holy Spirit in his life. It was before either my husband David or the missionary's wife had enjoyed such experience. We had stopped the car and were engrossed in conversation when suddenly two disturbing thoughts crossed my mind. The first was a warning St. Paul gave to 'be careful to do what is right in the eyes of everybody'. I realised that someone we knew, seeing us together, could easily draw the wrong conclusions. The second was about the consequences of crossing, even innocently, the previously well-defined limits of our relationship. Both thoughts appalled me. I quickly extricated myself from the situation. Wise people are doing this all the time.

3 Thirdly, let's never be naive about our own capacity to sin however strong we may fancy ourselves to be. 'Pride goes before a fall' is a wise proverb. God has warned us that the human heart is deceitful and beyond cure. Many people have pronounced the famous last words, 'It could never happen to me'.

4 Fourthly, we must be careful not to lie to ourselves. It is very easy to deceive ourselves about the reality and consequences of our actions. How many people have crossed the boundaries which surrounded their workplace or church activities and when questioned have excused it with, 'it's only platonic'.

   Others have foolishly crossed the proper boundaries and have then convinced themselves it must be all right because 'it feels good'. Another incredible excuse I have heard is: 'If it isn't right, why doesn't God stop us?' As if God treats us as puppets. [4]

46

Chapter 5
Enthusiasm

Doing Great

Nothing great has ever been achieved without enthusiasm. Ralph Waldo Emerson, the American writer and poet, put it well:

> Every great and commanding movement in the annals of the world is the triumph of enthusiasm.

The same is true concerning the future. Nothing great will be accomplished by any individual or group without enthusiasm.

Enthusiasm comes from the Greek word *en theos* and literally means 'in God'. The Oxford dictionary defines enthusiasm as 'ardent or burning zeal'. Zeal means earnestness or fervour in advancing a cause or rendering service.

The founder of Methodism, John Wesley (1703-1791), had the zeal of the Lord. For him it was an attitude and a way of life. He believed that the world was his parish. He had a travelling preaching ministry that included an annual tour of England and twenty visits to both Scotland and Ireland. He covered an estimated 250,000 miles, mostly on horseback and preached 40,000 sermons. He kept a detailed journal of his tours, wrote commentaries on Scripture and edited classical works. Wesley said:

> I have one aim in view, to beget, preserve and increase the life of God in the soul of man.

His ambition was, 'to reform the nation and spread scriptural holiness throughout the land'. With godly enthusiasm Wesley preached Christ, changing the lives of thousands of people. He said:

Do all the good you can, in all the ways you can, in all the places you can, at all the times you can, to all the people you can, as long as ever you can. [1]

Your Enthusiasm Stirs

The Apostle Paul, writing to the Christians at Corinth, was thankful that their enthusiasm had such an amazing effect.

> *For I know your eagerness to help and I have been boasting about it to the Macedonians telling them that since last year, you in Achaia, were ready to give and your enthusiasm has stirred most of them to action* (2 Corinthians 9:2).

The enthusiasm of the Christians in Achaia was such that it stirred up the churches in Philippi, Thessalonica and Berea to give financially and sacrificially to help the impoverished believers in Jerusalem. Paul was now asking the Corinthian Church to complete the collection that they had begun as it had apparently slowed down or had come to a standstill. He took it upon himself to assist in gathering this collection and its delivery through the safe hands of Titus, fellow worker and assistant to Paul in his missionary work. It was the Corinthian's zeal in giving, that had started and motivated the other collections. Enthusiasm is infectious. It stirs up others to take action.

Iron Sharpens Iron

During the spring of 1995 I spent ten days at the Christ for all Nations (CfaN), 'Fire Conference' in Addis Ababa in Ethiopia. I wanted to learn as much as I could from evangelist Reinhard Bonnke, the founder and director of CfaN. The purpose of the conference was to equip and motivate the ten thousand Christians gathered, of whom the majority were in leadership, in effectively sharing the gospel of Christ. The wonderful Ethiopians gathered daily to hear Reinhard Bonnke teach. The reason he spoke so effectively was because he spoke with enthusiasm and passion. The reason for the zeal for God and people is simple: Reinhard is in love with those he ministers to. The hearts and lives of the Ethiopian Christians were stirred for action.

On returning to England I found I was different. My passion for God increased. His calling on my life as an ambassador for Christ, proclaiming the good news was ignited afresh. I was fired up.

Do not put out the Spirit's fire (1 Thessalonians 5:19).

Author and speaker, Skip Ross writes:

Enthusiasm is one of the keys for success in our growing vibrant churches today. [2]

Whatever your hands find to do, do it with all your might (Ecclesiastes 9:10).

Jesus Gentle and Zealous

In the Temple courts Jesus found some people selling cattle, sheep and doves; others were sitting at tables exchanging money. The outer courts were the one place that Gentiles could come to pray and worship. However, these courts had become a noisy, smelly marketplace; the Jewish religious leaders were interfering with the provision God had made for the Gentiles.

What was Jesus' response? John, who was one of Christ's closest disciples, records:

He made a whip out of cords, and drove all from the temple area, both sheep and cattle; he scattered the coins of the moneychangers and overturned their tables. To those who sold doves He said, 'Get these out of here! How dare you turn my Father's house into a market!' His disciples remembered that it is written, 'Zeal for your house will consume me.' (John 2:15-17)

Our Lord Jesus is zealous. Our God is zealous, accomplishing his purposes.

> For to us a child is born, to us a son is given, and the government will be on his shoulders. And he will be called Wonderful Counsellor, Mighty God, Everlasting Father, Prince of Peace. Of the increase of his government and peace there will be no end. He will reign on David's throne and over his kingdom, establishing and upholding it with justice and righteousness from that time on and for ever. The zeal of the Lord Almighty will accomplish this (Isaiah 9:6-7).

Nothing great was or ever will be accomplished without godly enthusiasm and zeal. Enthusiasm can be cultivated. Enthusiasm makes ordinary people extraordinary. You can make a difference. Edward Hale said:

> I am only one, but I *am* one. I can't do everything, but I *can* do something. And what I *can* do, that I ought to do. And what I *ought* to do, by the grace of God, I *shall* do. [3]

Chapter 6
Faith

No one can please God without faith. Whoever comes to God must have faith that he exists. He rewards those who seek him. To have faith is to be certain of the things we hope for, to be sure of the things we cannot see.

In Bible times a person's faith won God's approval (Hebrews 11:1-2,6). We understand that faith matters, to us and to God. Our faith affects those around us. It affects the situations we encounter. Talk of faith and trusting is good, but for some people it brings despair. They know a certain level or quality of faith is required, but they cannot reach it. They wrongly think that their prayers are feeble, that God is not pleased with their lack of faith or trust. Some struggle with faith because they find trusting difficult. Others are suspicious and doubtful. Some feel that God has let them down, so to trust him for a better day is almost impossible. This feeling that God has let them down affects their demeanour and their walk as a Christian. It can affect everything.

When I preach in Africa one thing becomes very clear. Faith seems to fill the air. You can see faith written on the hearts and minds of people. The people listen to the messages with expectancy. Anything could happen and it often does. There the Church really does believe that Jesus is the same yesterday, today and forever as the Bible states in Hebrews 13:8. They have faith because they believe that healings and miracles occur. Sadly the same is not true in Britain. Most of us are cursed with a sense of the impossible and that is precisely why miracles do not happen. It seems to me that those who regard themselves as having weak trust in God do themselves an enormous injury. They disqualify themselves when God does not. Jesus said:

'Whoever comes to me, I will never drive away.' (John 6:37)

Faith Cries Out

One day a man came to Jesus with faith that was feeble and weak. However, he cried out for mercy with all the faith that he could and Jesus granted his request (Mark 9:14-29). The man had first brought his son to the disciples to be healed.

They tried to heal the boy but could not. An argument broke out between the disciples and the teachers of the Law over the lack of healing. When Jesus came on the scene the situation began to change. The father of the boy explained to Jesus that the disciples were ineffective in driving the evil spirit out of his son.

Jesus asked the father how long the boy had suffered.

> *'From childhood,' he answered. 'It has often thrown him into fire or water to kill him. But if you can do anything, take pity on us and help us.'*
> *'If you can?' said Jesus. 'Everything is possible for the person who has faith.'*

Jesus stated the conditions needed for the miracle. It was as if Jesus said, 'The cure of the boy depends, not on me, but on you.' The father could hardly cope with this demand of faith. In anguish he cried out to Jesus, 'I do have faith, but not enough. Help me have more.' Was that good enough for Jesus? Did he accept the faith of the father even though it was inadequate and weak? The answer is a definite yes, even though the prayer, 'Help us, if you possibly can' was most feeble. The father was helpless. Jesus was not going to turn him away. The father came to Jesus and asked for help. His faith was faltering, but Christ accepted the father and healed the boy.

This is the most important aspect of prayer, important because it gives boldness in our approach even when our faith is weak. Jesus receives those who come however faltering or helpless. Those coming in such condition are not a problem to Him. He does not reject those with an apparent lack of faith. The problem occurs because a lack of faith or being helpless is a problem to us. It hinders us, but it should not. It is a shame that Christians rule themselves out when Christ would not do so. A Christian's helplessness is what gets him heard by the living Lord Jesus. Helplessness qualifies us in the eyes of Christ.

Winning Faith

Victory is won by means of our faith. Those who believe in Jesus, the Son of God, can defeat the world and everything it throws at us. Sometimes what we might regard defeat is a victory in God's eyes. Even Christians consider death to be a defeat. The death of a respected Christian leader is viewed as a tragedy. We tend to look at suffering as unacceptable. We say, 'Surely this can't be God's plan for us'.

There is a list of heroes mentioned in the book of Hebrews who, through faith, got the victory (Hebrews 11:32-35). They won. They fought and won, shut the mouths of lions, put out fierce fires, escaped being killed by the sword, and received their dead relatives back to life. There was another group of godly people who were defeated and lost, until you read what God thought about it. For God, it was victory.

> *Others, refusing to accept freedom, died under torture in order to be raised to a better life. Some were mocked and whipped, and others were put in chains and taken off to prison. They were stoned, they were sawn in two, they were killed by the sword. They went around clothed in skins of sheep or goats - poor, persecuted, and ill-treated. The world was not good enough for them! They wandered like refugees in the deserts and hills, living in caves and holes in the ground* (Hebrews 11:35b-38, Good News Bible).

In conclusion all those mentioned won by faith, even those who died or who suffered terribly. There are no losers on God's side. We must understand that apparent defeat is often not defeat at all.

> *What a record all these have won by their faith! Yet they did not receive what God had promised, because God had decided on an even better plan for us. His purpose was that only in company with us would they be made perfect* (Hebrews 11:39-40, Good News Bible).

Being faithful is costly. It cost Abraham the giving up of his only son. It cost Esther the risk of her life. It cost Daniel being cast into the lion's den. It cost Stephen death by stoning. It cost Peter a martyr's death. It cost Paul his life. Does it cost you and me anything to be faithful to our Lord?

Leap of Faith

God is often speaking to his people. He speaks in many different ways. We are familiar with some of them; through people, the Bible, dreams or visions, nature, circumstances, and the Holy Spirit. Often He tells us something that is contrary to our thinking. He sometimes asks us to do something for him or for others that may come as a surprise. He is the God of surprises. As we journey through life we must always be ready to hear and obey. As the old hymn says:

> *Trust and obey*
> *For there's no other way*
> *To be happy in Jesus*
> *Than to trust and obey.*

Have faith in God. Obey the prompting of the Holy Spirit. Whatever He tells you to do, do it.

One of the biggest leaps of faith that I had ever taken happened while I was on a preaching visit to Nigeria. While I was seated on the platform with my colleagues from England, I knew I had to make a decision to 'step out of the safety of the boat', out of my comfort zone. It was a decision made under the direction of the Holy Spirit.

In front of me were many hundreds of Nigerian Christians at Christ Apostolic Church, Agbala Itura (Vineyard of Comfort),

Ibadan. It was a hot spring evening. I felt a boldness welling up inside. My faith in God was strong. It was a daring faith. The kind that puts your faith on the line. The congregation was expectant for miracles. When I had finished the message I called people forward with specific illnesses. Hundreds came forward. The British team with the Nigerian church leaders went out to these people, laying hands on many and praying for healing. A woman caught my eye. I went over to her and continued to pray for her until I felt she was healed. Something came out of her body. Another person I prayed for was finally delivered from evil spirits at the end of a loud, intense prayer time. People came forward and shared how they had been healed and delivered during the prayer time.

Another time a young evangelist named Joseph was ill. The Lord told me what to do. I telephoned and told him I was sending a handkerchief that he was to place under his pillow for three nights. He did this and was healed.

I Believe I Can Fly
by R. Kelly

I used to think that I could not go on
And life was nothing but an awful song
But now I know the meaning of true love
I'm leaning on the Everlasting Arms

If I can see it
Then I can do it
If I just believe it
There's nothing to it

I believe I can fly
I believe I can touch the sky
I think about it every night and day
Spread my wings and fly away
I believe I can soar
I see me running through that open door
I believe I can fly

I believe I can fly
I believe I can fly

See I was on the verge of breaking down
Sometimes silence can seem so loud
There are miracles in life I must achieve
But first I know it starts inside of me

Oh if I see it
Then I can be it
If I just believe it
There's nothing to it

I believe I can fly
I believe I can touch the sky
I think about it every night and day
Spread my wings and fly away
I believe I can soar
I see me running through that open door
I believe I can fly
I believe I can fly
I believe I can fly

Cause I believe in You

If I can see it
Then I can do it
If I just believe it
There's nothing to it

I believe I can fly
I believe I can touch the sky
I think about it every night and day
Spread my wings and fly away
I believe I can soar
I see me running through that open door
I believe I can fly
I believe I can fly

I believe I can fly

If I just spread my wings
I can fly
I can fly
I can fly

The story is told of a blind boy who was flying a kite and enjoying this pastime along with others of his own age. A passer-by, knowing him and wanting to give him a gentle teasing, said, 'Where is your kite? You don't know whether it is on the ground or up in the sky.'

'Oh yes,' said the boy, 'I do know. It is now quite a fair height up in the air.'

'How do you know that?' asked his friend, 'You can't see it.'

'No!' replied the boy, 'I can't see it, it is true, but I can feel the tug of the string.' [1]

Chapter 7

Gifts

You Are Talented

In Matthew 25:14-30 we read that there was a certain man about to go on a journey. He called his servants and put them in charge of his property. He gave to each one according to his ability. One servant received five talents, another two and the other one. This parable that Jesus told has vital lessons for us today.

The term 'talent' was understood as a unit of coinage. One talent was the same as 1,000 gold coins. The talents were entrusted to the three servants. It was their responsibility and opportunity to make money for their master. The servant who had five talents put his money to work and earned five more. Similarly the servant who had two talents earned two more. But the servant who had been given one talent dug a hole in the ground and hid it.

After a long time the master returned and settled accounts with them. He congratulated the first two servants and rewarded them with gifts because of their faithfulness in managing that which they had been given. The servant who was given one talent tried to justify himself by saying, *'Master I know that you are a hard man harvesting where you have not sown and gathering where you have not scattered seed. So I was afraid and went out and hid your talent in the ground. See, here is what belongs to you.'* (Matthew 25:24-25) The master was not pleased with this and told his servant that he was lazy and bad. He asked him why he did not put the talent to some use by placing it in the bank to receive interest. The one talent was removed from the servant and given to the one who had ten.

Jesus explained the meaning of the parable saying:

' *"For everyone who has will be given more, and he will have an abundance. Whoever does not have, even what he has will be taken from him. And throw that worthless*

servant outside, into darkness, where there will be weep-
ing and gnashing of teeth".' (Matthew 25:29-30)

Jesus uses the term talent to indicate an ability or gift given
to an individual.

There are three important principles to note and follow:

1   Each and every Christian is given a gift. God has given us
    time, gifts and other resources. He expects us to put them
    to good use. No-one is excluded. Jesus, like the master in
    the parable, is wise and discerning to know what to give.
    No Christian receives no more or less than could be han-
    dled. If we fail in our task our excuse can not be that we
    are overwhelmed. The lack of success may be because of
    laziness or disobedience.

2   Fear can stop us. The servant said to the master, '*So I was*
    afraid and went out and hid your talent in the ground.'
    (Matthew 25:25) Fear prevented the servant using the tal-
    ent he was given. He was obsessed with safety and secu-
    rity. Do not bury your talent. Use your God-given gifts to
    advance the Kingdom of God and to do good. Do not be
    afraid. Many Christians have stopped or have not started
    to use their gifts or talents. Our time, abilities or money
    is not ours - we are caretakers, not owners. Christians
    must not ignore, squander or abuse what they have; inac-
    tion for whatever reason is inappropriate. Leonardo Da
    Vinci said, 'Iron rusts from disuse, stagnant water looses
    its purity, and in cold weather becomes frozen, even so
    does inaction sap the vigours of the mind.'[1]

3   A wrong view of someone or something hinders. The servant
    had a wrong view and relationship with his master. '*Master, I*
    knew that you are a hard man...' (Matthew 25:24) This
    together with the fear he possessed prevented the servant
    from using his talent. There are those who have a poor and
    inadequate relationship with God. This does not have to be.
    For Christians God is Abba - Father. He is compassionate and

loving towards his children. The kind of fear we should have of God is one of respect and honour, not a dreadful terrifying fear. The servant would have done better if his beliefs and relationship with his master was like that described below:

The Lord is compassionate and gracious,
slow to anger, abounding in love.
He will not always accuse,
nor will he harbour his anger for ever;
He does treat us as our sins deserve
or repay us according to our iniquities.
For as high as the heavens are above the earth,
so great is his love for those who fear him;
For he knows how we are formed,
he remembers that we are dust. (Psalm 103:8-16)

Whether you are a five, two or one talent person does not matter. You are gifted.

Talents are distributed unevenly, it is true - to one ten, to another five, but each has one pound, all alike. [2] (R. H. Benson)

The tragedy of life is not being limited to one talent, but in the failure to use the one talent. [3] (Edgar W. Work)

Spiritual Gifts

Jesus operated in the power of the Holy Spirit. He was endowed with spiritual gifts. The four Gospels clearly show that his three years of public ministry included healings, miracles, deliverance, and prophecy. Many people were set free and given a new start because of the manifestation of the Holy Spirit working through him. The Apostle Paul was also able to heal because he allowed the spiritual gifts to flow through him. Paul encouraged believers to do the same in order that the Church would be built up and made stronger. Paul instructed the church at Corinth to follow the way of love and eagerly desire the spiritual gifts (see 1 Corinthians 12:31; 14:1).

For the Good of All

There are different kinds of gifts. There are gifts of wisdom, knowledge, faith, healing, miracles, prophecy, discernment or distinguishing between spirits, speaking in different kinds of tongues, and the interpretation of tongues (1 Corinthians 12:8-10). The Holy Spirit gives these spiritual gifts to each one for the common good. The Spirit gives these to each one just as he determines (1 Corinthians 12:4-8).

Believers must pursue the way of love and eagerly desire the spiritual gifts if these manifestations are to occur in us and through us. Paul says to the Christians in Corinth:

> *Since you are eager to have spiritual gifts, try to excel in gifts that build up the church* (1 Corinthians 14:12).

Again and again Paul spells it out that the edification, strengthening and encouragement of the church is of great importance in the exercise of the spiritual gifts (1 Corinthians 14:4-6, 12-17, 26-31).

In addition to these gifts of the Holy Spirit there are the gifts of Christ. Apostles, prophets, evangelists, pastors and teachers exist to equip the church for service and build up the Church (Ephesians 4:11-12).

The seven gifts of God are listed by Paul: prophecy, serving, teaching, encouraging, giving (to the need of others), leadership, and showing mercy (Romans 12:6-8).

A Myth Exists

Paul paints a picture when he likens the Church to the human body. The Church has many parts, with Christ as its head. The body is not made up of only one part, but of many parts.

There are Christians who despise themselves and say they do not belong to the rest of the Church - the body of believers; because they are not like somebody else.

> *'Because I am not a hand I do not belong to the body...'*
> (1 Corinthians 12:15)

This is unnecessary and unhelpful. It is self persecution. Unfortunately there are those within the church that reject their brother or sister by saying they are not needed.

> *The eye cannot say to the hand, 'I do not need you!'*
> (1 Corinthians 12:21)

A myth exists. I have heard it said that no-one is indispensable. Paul says the opposite. He dispels the myth and puts the record straight when he says:

> *On the contrary, those parts of the body that seem to be weaker are indispensable* (1 Corinthians 12:22).

There are those in churches that are of paramount importance. Do not be surprised that these are the weaker members. They are important to God, his church and his Kingdom. We cannot do without the weaker members. They are indispensable. The Bible says so. Paul goes on to say that the parts that we think are less honourable or not worth much we should treat with special honour. The parts that are unpresentable or obscure should be treated with special modesty.

You are gifted. What is your gift and contribution?

Gift of Giving

The early Church was a caring and sharing community. The Church in Jerusalem was over three thousand strong. The Christians spent their time learning from the Apostles and taking part in the fellowship. They shared meals and broke bread remembering the death of Christ. They were committed to prayer and to each other. The Apostles performed miracles and wonders in the name of Jesus by the power of the Holy Spirit. The believers continued together in close fellowship and shared their belongings. Of the early church it is stated,

> ... *selling their possessions and goods, they gave to any-one as he had need* (Acts 2:45).

As time went on the Church continued to be a loving fellow-ship. The believers were of one heart and mind. The Christians did not claim that their possessions were their own to hold on to, but they shared with anyone who had need. There were no needy people in the church because from time to time those who owned fields or houses would sell them and donate the money from the sale to the Apostles. This was then distributed to each according to their need (Acts 4:32-35). This amazing behaviour was volun-tary. It did not involve all private property, only that which was needed. It was not a condition of membership into the church.

From the sale of his books alone John Wesley gave away about £40,000. When he died, his personal estate amounted to only a few pounds. When earning £30 a year, he lived on £28 and gave the remaining £2 to the Lord's work. The next year his salary was doubled. He found that he lived comfortably on £28 a year, so, instead of raising his standard of living, he continued to live on £28 a year and gave the whole of his increase to God. So later God entrusted him with larger and larger amounts.

What we give is very much up to us. There is great need in the world and the church. God has a bias toward the poor and needy. It is our responsibility and privilege to help those who are destitute, poor or needy. The early church was extremely gener-ous. We also need to have open hearts and pockets to do what-ever we can. We must be open to the Holy Spirit, to do what he says. In the Bible there is a principle of tithing, giving ten percent of your income to God. Everything we have is God's. Let's be generous with our time, our talents and our tithes.

In my visits to Nigeria and Ethiopia I have seen great poverty where inflation is high. Despite this the Christians give gener-ously. For them giving to God's work is as important as wor-shipping God; it is part of their worship. Several collections in one meeting are common. There is joy written on their faces as they give. In such places revival has occurred and continues.

Chapter 8
Holy Spirit

The Holy Spirit is a counsellor, comforter and a divine helper. Jesus Christ promised his disciples that they were going to experience a baptism with the Holy Spirit. Jesus told them he was going away, back to God, but that he would give them the Holy Spirit. Jesus always addressed the Holy Spirit as him or he, never as it (John 14:15-17; 16:5-11).

The Holy Spirit is a very powerful person. He is not a force. The Holy Spirit has personality. He speaks, guides and can be grieved (Ephesians 4:30). Fellowship and friendship with the Holy Spirit is encouraged (Philippians 2:1). Paul concludes his second letter to the church in Corinth by praying this prayer for them:

May the grace of the Lord Jesus Christ, and the love of God and the fellowship of the Holy Spirit be with you all (2 Corinthians 13:14).

Jesus told Nicodemus that he must be born again if he was to enter the kingdom of God; born again of the Holy Spirit (John 3:3-8). Jesus explained to Nicodemus that as he had had a physical birth, so he must have a spiritual birth through the Holy Spirit.

The Holy Spirit is the Spirit of truth. The Holy Spirit is the Spirit of Jesus, that is, he is the same in character as Jesus. The Holy Spirit is the third person of the Trinity. There is only one God. God-the-Father, God-the-Son (that is, Jesus), and God-the-Holy Spirit; three distinct persons.

When the Holy Spirit controls the life of the believer he produces these qualities: love, joy, peace, patience, kindness, goodness, faithfulness, gentleness, and self-control (Galatians 5:22-

23). The Holy Spirit gives gifts to Christians as and when he decides, as we earnestly desire him and have fellowship with him. He gives wisdom, knowledge, faith, healings, miraculous powers, prophecy, the ability to distinguish between spirits, the speaking in tongues and the interpretation of tongues (1 Corinthians 12:7-10).

The Holy Spirit and Jesus

Jesus was anointed by the Holy Spirit. He was able to heal, deliver people from evil spirits, do the miraculous, and teach and preach powerfully bringing help and relief. Jesus walked and talked with the Holy Spirit. Jesus did amazing things because of the Holy Spirit's power in and through him.

John the Baptist appeared to prepare the way for Jesus. John instructed people to repent and get ready for the coming of the Christ. John baptised those who repented in the River Jordan. The water signified being cleansed from sin and new life. John said this of Jesus, '*I baptise you with water. But one more powerful than I will come, the thongs of whose sandals I am not worthy to untie. He will baptise you with the Holy Spirit and with fire.*' (Luke 3:15-16) Jesus experienced the tremendous power of the Holy Spirit. After the resurrection Jesus baptised others with the Holy Spirit and with fire.

John baptised Jesus in water. While Jesus was praying the heavens opened and the Holy Spirit came down on him in the form of a dove. A voice came from heaven that said:

> '*You are my Son, whom I love; with you I am well pleased.*' (Luke 3:21-22)

Jesus returned from the Jordan full of the Holy Spirit. He was led into the desert by the Holy Spirit. There he was tempted by the Devil for forty days (Luke 4:1-2). Jesus went to Galilee in the power of the Spirit. The whole countryside heard about Jesus. He travelled around, teaching in the synagogues. Everyone praised him (Luke 4:14-19). He went to Nazareth, the town where he had grown up. On the Sabbath he went to the synagogue. The scroll of the prophet Isaiah was handed to him. He carefully unrolled it and found the place where it said:

> *'The Spirit of the Lord is on me,*
> *because He has anointed me*
> *to preach good news to the poor.*
> *He has sent me to proclaim freedom*
> *for the prisoners*
> *and recovery of sight for the blind,*
> *to release the oppressed,*
> *to proclaim the year of the Lord's favour.'*
> (Luke 4:17-19)

He rolled up the scroll, gave it back to the attendant and sat down. Everyone looked at him, waiting and wondering. Jesus said to them:

> *'Today this scripture is fulfilled in your hearing.'*

Jesus announced that he was going to fulfil these things. He was going to bring healing, deliverance and salvation. Jesus did just that. Through his life and ministry the Spirit of God was on him. He was anointed by the Holy Spirit. Jesus drove out evil spirits from people (Luke 4:31-37; 8:26-39; 9:37-46; 11:14-28). Jesus healed many (Luke 4:38-39). He healed those with leprosy (Luke 5:12-16). He healed a paralytic (Luke 5:17-26). He healed the dying centurion's servant (Luke 7:1-10). He raised a widow's son back to life (Luke 7:11-17). He raised a dead girl to life and healed a sick woman (Luke 8:14-56). Jesus multiplied a few loaves and fish to feed 5,000 hungry men, plus women and children(Luke 9:10-17). He healed ten lepers (Luke 17:11-19).

Jesus' teaching on the Holy Spirit

One day whilst praying in a certain place one of Jesus' disciples asked him if he would teach them to pray. Jesus taught them the Lord's prayer. He told them to ask, seek and knock, emphasising that they were to persevere in prayer. To finish he said these words:

'Which of you fathers, if your son asks for a fish, will give him a snake instead? Or if he asks for an egg, will give him a scorpion? If you then, though you are evil, know how to give good gifts to your children, how much more will your Father in heaven give the Holy Spirit to those who ask Him!' (Luke 11:11-13)

Jesus told his disciples that his Father wanted to give them the Holy Spirit, a good gift to all those who ask. The only condition was to ask. There is no question whether God will or will not give the Holy Spirit. The Counsellor, who is our helper and comforter, is available to us. He will teach us all things and will remind us of the words of Jesus. He will empower us. Be full of the Holy Spirit. Allow the Holy Spirit to direct and guide you.

The Holy Spirit and Me

Immediately after becoming a Christian I attended an excellent Youth Fellowship. The Saturday sports and games evening were most enjoyable. The Sunday evening meetings were extremely helpful to me as a young Christian. The speakers, Bible studies, worship and prayer times were instrumental in my formation as a follower of Jesus. I made new friends. Roger and Katie, our Youth Leaders, became my spiritual parents. They were people I could trust. They helped me to know Christ better.

After attending for six months they organised a holiday in the country for the group. It was a wonderful opportunity to get to know others, have fun and enjoy the Lord's presence. I did not know that something significant was going to happen to me during this time away. The theme of the week was 'the Holy Spirit in the life of the Believer'. I asked the guest speakers about the baptism of the Holy Spirit. They suggested I went away and ask God to baptise me with his Holy Spirit. They promised that they would pray for me also.

I prayed for the next two days. I remember being apart from the others to pray. I sensed that something was about to happen. I sat on top of a hill praying. As I looked down at the trees, fields and river at the bottom of the hill, I was praying for the baptism with the Holy Spirit. One night we returned to our dormitories to sleep. As I lay on the top bunk I asked God again to give me the baptism with the Holy Spirit and to change me. As I lay praying, joy came pouring into me, a joy that I had never experienced before. I experienced the love of Christ for me at the cross. I felt Christ's love. The joy was so great that I could not sleep. I asked God to take some of the joy away so that I could sleep. I finally fell asleep. That night God baptised me in his Holy Spirit.

The next day I told my youth leaders what had happened. They were delighted. There was an immediate difference in my life. I had an overwhelming desire and ability to share the good news of Jesus and my story of knowing Christ with others. I shared with friends and strangers. A power and boldness to witness effectively followed. There were several people that I had known for a long time who became Christians and started to go to church through my witness. I felt the Lord closer to me than ever before. The Bible had greater meaning and was increasingly relevant. I enjoyed praying immensely. For me Christianity was about knowing Christ and making him known. Since my baptism with the Holy Spirit making him known was a privilege and challenge.

> *Every time we say 'I believe in the Holy Spirit, we mean that we believe there is a living God able and willing to enter human personality and change it.'* [1] (J. B. Phillips)

After his resurrection Jesus told his disciples to wait in Jerusalem until the Holy Spirit came on them. He made it clear that they were not to take the gospel to anyone until they had received the baptism with the Holy Spirit (Luke 24:45-49; Acts 1:7-8). They waited for the Holy Spirit.

When the Holy Spirit came, it was the Jewish feast of Pentecost, and the disciples were together in one place. Suddenly a sound like a violent wind came from heaven and filled the house. They saw what seemed to be tongues of fire that separated and came to rest on each of them. Each of them was baptised or filled with the Holy Spirit and spoke with other languages or tongues, as the Spirit enabled them (Acts 2:1-4).

A large crowd had gathered to see what the noise and excite-ment were about. Peter spoke to them about Jesus. Around 3,000 people heard his message, repented of their sins and were baptised in water. These new believers joined the Church. The difference that the outpouring of the Holy Spirit made on the disciples in the upper room was obvious. The Christians had the power to witness effectively, just as Jesus had said.

The baptism with the Holy Spirit is given to equip Christians with boldness and power to share Christ.

R. A. Torey had been a minister for years when the Holy Spirit came upon him. He says:

> I recall the exact spot where I was kneeling in prayer in my study … It was a very quiet moment, one of the most quiet moments I ever knew … Then God simply said to me, not in any audible voice, but in my heart, 'It's yours. Now go and preach.' He had already said it to me in his Word in 1 John 5:14-15; but I did not then know my Bible as I know it now, and God had pity on my ignorance and said it directly to my soul … I went and preached, and I have been a new minister from that day to this … Some time after this experience (I do not recall just how long after), while sitting in my room one day … suddenly … I found myself shouting (I was not brought up to shout and I am not of a shouting temperament, but I shouted like the loudest shouting Methodist), 'Glory to God, glory to God, glory to God', and I could not stop… But that was not when I was baptised with the Holy Spirit. I was baptised with the Holy Spirit when I took him by simple faith in the Word of God. [2]

How did D. L. Moody, the great American evangelist, feel and act when the Holy Spirit of God came upon him, transforming his life and ministry?

> I was crying all the time that God would fill me with His Spirit. Well, one day, in the city of New York - oh, what a day! I cannot describe it, I seldom refer to it; it is almost

too sacred an experience to name. Paul had an experience of which he never spoke for fourteen years. I can only say that God revealed himself to me, and I had such an experience of his love that I had to ask him to stay his hand. I went preaching again. The sermons were not different; I did not present any new truths; and yet hundreds were converted. I would not now be placed back where I was before that blessed experience if you should give me all the world - it would be as the small dust of the balance. [3]

Charles Finney had an experience when the Holy Spirit came upon him and changed him for ever:

I received a mighty baptism of the Holy Spirit without any expectation of it, without ever having the thought in my mind that there was any such thing for me, without any recollection that I had ever heard the thing mentioned by any person in the world, the Holy Spirit descended upon me in a manner that seemed to go through me body and soul. No words can express the wonderful love that was shed abroad in my heart. I wept aloud with joy and love. [4]

Chapter 9

Interface

During a long flight to Lagos on a preaching trip to Nigeria, I spent many hours being interviewed by publicist Phil Dowding, one of my team on that occasion. Afterwards, he wrote about some of the issues that matter to me:

At 10.00 p.m., one day in July 1973, Andy Economides was born again. A friend of his called Kevin Lambert - who wasn't even a believer - took him along to a summer camp in Limpsfield, Surrey, and they both heard a message that changed their lives. He can't remember the exact day, but knows that it was the start of a new life. And soon began the burning passion to see people come to Christ began.

There is a distinct Mediterranean look about him and his name isn't very British, which is hardly surprising with both his parents Greek Cypriots who came to London before he was born.

Andy has strong opinions on the state of the Church today, having experienced it in several countries around the world and seeing both rapid growth, like in Nigeria, and fairly static situations as in Britain. He says one of the greatest needs for the church in any country is good leadership.

The leaders of the group are key people; if you have bad leadership, everything begins to deteriorate. Integrity is very important for them. They must be people who are honest, transparent and secure (if you have a leader who isn't secure then you can have some very serious problems). And we need to see the leaders in our churches willing to pass things on to others, to be more creative, to prefer others, and to create space for individuals. The church needs to be more flexible. Then we'll see a steady rise in the spirituality of local churches.

When asked why churches and individuals in Britain on the whole are not involved in evangelism, he groans at the thought of it.

They have done so little of it (or none of it, in many cases) that it has become a way of life not to. It's a habit now, and as our habits help make up our characters, its going to take something big to break a lifelong habit of not sharing the Gospel.

I believe passionately that every Christian can share their faith in Jesus, and God can help them.

'The problem is with us - not God', he says. He groans again when Christians say: 'Well, its not my gift, I'm a worship leader', or 'I put the flowers in the church', or 'I clean the carpet'. And when they say: 'I'm not an evangelist, that's not my calling, that's not my gifting', or 'I'm too shy', because he knows that Jesus said to his disciples: 'You are my witnesses'.

We are either good witnesses or bad witnesses.

He applauds the major initiatives that churches have instigated over the last few years, but insists that the best way is for every local church to get its act together and do local and personal evangelism.

If every local church had a mission each year and helped train its members in evangelism, the effect would be enormous. I think churches should set an evangelism budget of ten percent of its income for the task. Many give to foreign missions (and so they should), but there are very few churches that are really effective in evangelism in their own locality.

Churches could be very very creative, but most Christians are frightened when it comes to evangelism. So we have to overcome our fears. We have to be confident in God, in ourselves and in the Gospel. Many in Britain are not tremendously confident in the Gospel.

The Apostle Paul wasn't ashamed of the Gospel because it was the power of God. I believe that there is inherent power in the Gospel itself and so when I share it with someone, I have confidence in that power. We have to get back to basics and believe what the Bible says about the Gospel.

Fond memories for Andy include the obvious (but real) stuff about when he asked Annette to marry him, his conversion, and when Hannah their daughter was born. Another turning point for him; he went to watch Reinhard Bonnke in Addis Ababa in 1995, to see how he did things, what he spoke about, to see the large crowds, to observe and learn from perhaps one of the greatest evangelists currently in the world, who preaches the Gospel to perhaps more people than anyone else at the moment.

He started visiting Nigeria (where he says his favourite Chinese restaurant is) in 1991 with Korky Davey, Bristol-based director of Open Air Campaigners of the West Country region. Since then he has returned many times and has developed a strong love for the people and strong ties with the Christian-run Prospect Secretarial College in Ibadan, where he has arranged free scholarships for poorer students. He is closely involved with the leaders of Christ Apostolic Church in Lagos and Ibadan cities - one of the country's largest churches with satellite churches around the country and even the world. Whenever he visits, he speaks at the annual Jesus Festival, which attracts up to 30,000 people each night.

Andy loves Prospect College. Set up by Pastor Samuel Folahan in 1984 to help people get jobs by first getting a qualification, it quickly gained recognition and approval from the government to offer certificates and diplomas. Since 1995, because of Andy, it has been affiliated to the University of Northumbria in Newcastle, England and now specialises in computing, accountancy, secretarial and basic studies. Student numbers vary from 600-800, with ages between 18 and 23. Almost all are female, because although some men in Nigeria become secretaries, women are faster at typing!

Now students come from all over Nigeria - Christianity is not a barrier to families of other religions because of the high status the college enjoys. The college doesn't take only Christians, but most of its students are converted - even Muslims. Each year it baptises around 50 people.

Between the five trips since Andy's first visit in 1991 he has helped source numerous used computers from Britain and set up scholarships for a growing number of poor students, who would not otherwise get the opportunity.

'What excites me is the future the college provides for its students, both spiritually and materially. Graduates not only get a job, but the large majority also find Jesus. I can't wait for a new college building on the outskirts of the city to be finished. It will make space for far more students in better accommodation and take the work on another stage'.

Sponsoring students has become one of his ventures in Britain and many people have joined the project to give young Nigerian adults an education - and therefore be in a better position to get a job and have a future. Andy dreams of a better Nigeria where hospitals are open to everyone, corruption is eliminated, and food is available to all.

A bit nearer to home, he commits time, energy and resources to encourage several young, emerging evangelists and leaders in Britain, and he wants to expand this mentoring work both in this country and overseas.

Andy is a proclaimer of good news, which he does with both passion and compassion, and it drives him to reach out to the lost. Thousands have gained hope in the Gospel of Jesus - and he's only just started.

Chapter 10

Jesus Heals A Paralytic

Deepest Needs

Jesus had travelled throughout Galilee preaching in the synagogues and driving out demons. He returned to Capernaum. The news of his coming spread quickly. In Jesus' day life in Palestine was very open. In the morning doors of houses were opened and anyone who wanted could go in and out. Doors were only shut if a person wished for privacy. In humbler houses there was no entrance hall because the door opened directly on to the street.

In Mark 2:1-12 Jesus was visiting such a house. In no time at all many gathered to see him. The house was completely full. There was no room left outside the house either. The crowd both inside and outside were now eagerly listening to the words of the teacher.

While this was happening four men carrying a paralysed friend on a stretcher approached the scene. The crowd prevented them from getting their friend to Jesus. They were determined and ingenious.

The roof of the house, like most houses at that time, was flat. The roof was often used as a place of rest and quiet so usually there was an outside staircase leading up to the roof. It consisted of flat beams laid across from wall to wall, about three feet apart. The spaces between the beams were filled with brush wood and then packed tight with clay. It was easy to dig out the packing between two of the beams. It would not damage the house and would be easy to repair.

The four men carried their friend up onto the roof. Once there, they dug out an opening, they lowered the paralysed man down directly in front of Jesus' feet. When Jesus saw this faith that laughed at barriers, he must have smiled. He looked at the paralysed man and said:

'Son, your sins are forgiven.'

This may seem an odd way to begin a cure, but Jesus had a purpose in forgiving his sins before healing him. The paralytic had an obvious outward need, a felt need. Jesus first met the man's deepest need of forgiveness. The sin and shame were gone. He was declared free. Forgiveness is man's deepest need and highest achievement. There is no condemnation, only love and forgiveness. Jesus knows our deepest needs better than we do.

I was preaching one Sunday morning, in Southern France, through an interpreter. I spoke about Adam and his need (Genesis 2:18-25).

> The Lord God said, 'It is not good for the man to be alone. I will make a helper suitable for him.'

Adam needed a helper that was suitable for him. Adam had God as a companion and friend, but God was not enough for Adam's needs. The wonderful creation that surrounded Adam was not enough. God was pleased to provide for him what he needed. Eve, a beautiful woman and suitable helpmate was given to Adam.

The woman who had interpreted for me approached me at the end of the meeting and expressed her relief at what I had said about God not being enough. The realisation that God is not enough could bring a completeness to her life. It was perfectly acceptable and proper to have another person other than God - to have the friendship and love of a man. This young woman was beginning to receive love and acceptance for her deepest need. God was perfectly happy to provide another friendship in her life. This would not conflict with her life with God, and her desire to put Jesus first.

The authentic Jesus of the gospel is concerned about the needs that matter most, our deepest needs. He is not only concerned about felt needs or obvious needs.

You Cannot do That

Some of the teachers of the law, sitting in the house where Jesus was declaring forgiveness to another, thought:

> *'Why does this fellow talk like that? He's blaspheming! Who can forgive sins but God alone?'*

In other words, 'What is that? He has no right to say that and do that. Who does he think he is - God? You cannot do that.' Jesus knew immediately what they were thinking, and threw out a challenge saying:

> *'Why are you thinking these things? Which is easier to say to the paralytic, "Your sins are forgiven," or to say "Get up, take your mat and walk?" '*

Before they could answer (and I do not believe they either could have or would have, because Jesus did not give them an opportunity), he answered his question, in his own unique and amazing way. He commanded the man to get up, take up his mat and go home. In full view of everyone the man got up and walked home. Everyone was amazed. None of them had ever seen anything like this.

Jesus now completed what he wanted to do in the life of this dear, unfortunate man. He was now healed of his sickness and forgiven of his sin and shame. He was free. His outward obvious felt need for physical healing was met by Jesus. His inner, deeper need of Christ's forgiveness was also met by Jesus. He was made whole.

Carried by Four Friends

Can you imagine it? There he was, paralysed, and the healer was in town. His problem was how to get to Jesus? It was a good thing for him that four good friends showed practical love. Love in action. They carried the lame man. They faced several obstacles. The large crowd prevented them getting near Jesus, but they were determined to see the matter through. It was an unusual thing to do, to climb the stairs and break the roof. They lowered their friend down using ropes. They were courageous, determined and above all, loving. When the paralysed man was in front of Jesus their job was done. They contributed well in getting their friend to the healer.

There have been occasions when friends have come to me and carried me. At times all of us need to be carried by others. There are those who refuse to allow themselves to be carried, to be helped by others. It may be because they pride themselves on getting along on their own. It may be because of pride. There is a great need in our day for individuals, groups and churches to be involved in carrying those who need assistance.

> *Some men came, bringing to him a paralytic, carried by four of them. Since they could not get him to Jesus because of the crowd, they made an opening in the roof above Jesus and, after digging through it, lowered the mat the paralysed man was lying on. When Jesus saw their faith, he said to the paralytic, 'Son, your sins are forgiven.'* (Mark 2:3-5)

Jesus was pleased to see the faith of all five men. He was pleased with the commitment and love shown, and rewarded them.

Life-giving Words

The crowds were attracted to Jesus because the words he preached gave life, hope and freedom. His words and his personality were like a magnet drawing people to him. Jesus continually promised things. He invited people to come. No other person in history has ever been able to do the same because there is no other person that could fulfil such offers. He was and is unique. Nothing has changed. This is the Good News. Listen to the life giving words of Jesus:

> 'Blessed are the poor in spirit,
> for theirs is the kingdom of heaven.
> Blessed are those who mourn,
> for they will be comforted.
> 'Blessed are the meek,
> for they will inherit the earth.
> Blessed are those who hunger and thirst for righteousness,

for they will be filled.
Blessed are the merciful,
for they will be shown mercy.
Blessed are the pure in heart,
for they will see God.' (Matthew 5:3-8)

To the weary Jesus says:

'Come to me, all you are weary and burdened, and I will give you rest.' (Matthew 11:28)

To the thirsty Jesus says:

'If anyone is thirsty, let him come to me and drink. Whoever believes in me, as the Scripture has said, streams of living water will flow from within him.' (John 7:37-38)

By this he meant the Spirit, whom those who believed in him were later to receive.

To those who want a living friendship with Jesus today, he says:

'Here I am! I stand at the door and knock. If anyone hears my voice and opens the door, I will come in and eat with him, and he with me.' (Revelation 3:20)

Jesus spoke on every issue of life that touches humanity. For example, he spoke helpfully and profoundly on murder, adultery, oaths, truthfulness, love for enemies, giving to the needy, prayer, how not to worry, why not to worry and judging others (Matthew 5, 6, 7). Jesus spoke about life and death issues. Seize the time. Let the words of the Saviour help you, guide you and empower you. Allow the Spirit of God with the word of Christ and the word of God to bless your heart and life. Seize the time.

Chapter 11

Keys That Open Doors

We all have keys. Keys open many things. Keys help us to keep thieves out and our property safe. Although small, keys can open large doors. There are different keys to open different doors.

Obedience

Obedience to God can lead to many blessings. Obedience to God's word can lead to miracles.

The prophet Elijah asked the widow at Zarephath for a little water and bread (1 Kings 17:7-16). The widow informed the prophet that she only had a small amount of oil and flour. She was gathering sticks to make a small meal for her son and herself. She was poor and told Elijah that this would be their last meal before they died of starvation. Elijah told her not to be afraid. He told her to go home and make him a small loaf of bread and then a meal for her son and herself. The prophet spoke God's word to the woman:

> 'For this is what the Lord, the God of Israel, says: "The jar of flour will not be used up and the jug of oil will not run dry until the day the Lord gives rain on the land."' (1 Kings 17:14)

The widow did just as Elijah had told her and there was enough food. Obedience led to her miracle.

> For the jar of flour was not used up and the jug of oil did not run dry, in keeping with the word of the Lord spoken by Elijah (1 Kings 17:16).

Obedience opens doors to God's care. Moses was leading Israel out of Egypt into the promised land (Exodus 15:22-27). After travelling for three days they arrived at Marah, where the water was bitter and unfit to drink. The people grumbled at Moses saying, *'What are we to drink?'* God told Moses to throw a stick into the water and it became fit to drink.

Through Moses God made an agreement with Israel:

> *'If you listen carefully to the voice of the Lord your God and do what is right in his eyes, if you pay attention to his commands and keep all his decrees, I will not bring on you any of the diseases I bought on the Egyptians, for I am the Lord, who heals you.'* (Exodus 15:26)

Soon after they arrived at Elim where there were twelve springs and palm trees. They camped there near the water, finding rest and refreshment. God's promise to care for Israel was on the condition of their obedience to his word. By submitting to God he will care for us.

James says that it is important to listen to God's word, but more important to obey it (James 1:22-25). Listening and doing will open doors for us.

Obedience has its many rewards. God's army in the time of Joel became mighty because of obedience:

> *Mighty are those who obey His command* (Joel 2:11).

Obedience can make us Mighty

Rev. David Yonggi Cho pastors one of the largest churches in the world in Seoul, South Korea. The church numbers several hundreds of thousands. He puts the church growth down to prayer and obedience. Obedience to God's word opens the doors to all kinds of growth.

The Pharisees in Jesus' day were outwardly very religious and obedient. Jesus warned His disciple not to be like the Pharisees. Outward obedience to the law without a change of heart would not open the door to the kingdom of God.

> *'For I tell you that unless your righteousness surpasses that of the Pharisees and the teachers of the law, you will certainly not enter the kingdom of heaven.'* (Matthew 5:20)

The Pharisees were happy to obey the laws outwardly without allowing God to change their hearts and attitudes. Outward obedience without the change of heart is inadequate for Christ. Selective obedience is disobedience. Whatever God tells you to do, do it. His will for us is good, pleasing and perfect. Christianity is not 'pick and choose your favourite sweetie'. Obedience is not always easy. There will be times when God will test us. He will give us grace to find a way through. His grace is sufficient in our weakness. We can find strength to obey.

In the garden of Gethsemane Jesus needed strength to go all the way to the cross. He needed strength to obey (Matthew 26:37-38). Jesus' strength to obey came from his close friendship with his heavenly Father. Your friendship with your Father in heaven is also your strength. He will help you to obey.

There may be times when we will have to choose between obeying God and other people. The apostles were persecuted for their faith. The religious authorities told them not to spread the name of Jesus. Peter and the other apostles were brought before the Sanhedrin, the religious council. They said to them:

'We must obey God rather than man!' (Acts 5:29)

In 1940, the order had gone out - incurables and the insane were no longer to be a burden on the Reich. Three high officials descended upon the Bethel institution (a huge hospital for epileptics and the mentally ill). 'Herr Pastor,' they said, 'the Fuehrer has decided that all these people must be gassed.' Von Bodelschwingh looked at them calmly. 'You can put me into a concentration camp, if you want; that is your affair. But as long as I am free you do not touch one of my patients. I cannot change to fit the times or the wishes of the Fuehrer. I stand under the orders from our Lord Jesus Christ.' [1]

Obedience is a key that will open doors. Disobedience will have the opposite effect - doors will remain closed or shut.

Confidence

Two qualities are necessary to succeed in sport - ability and confidence. When a professional footballer looses his confidence, his game and performance deteriorate.

One key to success is confidence. The Christian's confidence starts with what Jesus has already accomplished for each of us. Let these words from the Bible build your confidence:

> *Therefore, brothers, since we have confidence to enter the Most Holy Place by the blood of Jesus, by a new and living way opened for us through the curtain, that is, his body, and since we have a great priest over the house of God, let us draw near to God with a sincere heart in full assurance of faith, having our hearts sprinkled to cleanse us from guilty conscience and having our bodies washed with pure water.* (Hebrews 10:19-22)

When Jesus died on the cross the curtain in the temple, which separated the people from the Holy of Holies - the Presence of God - was torn from top to bottom (Matthew 27:51, Hebrews 10:19-25). Jesus tore down the barrier between God and us. We can have boldness and confidence to freely approach our heavenly Father in prayer. It is a new and living way. It is the new covenant or agreement that God made between himself and us. Jesus' death on the cross gives us confidence in prayer. This permeates all areas of our lives.

Christians can be the most bold and confident people on earth. Be bold, be strong, for the Lord your God is with you. Your confidence is in the finished work of Jesus Christ, the Son of God.

Confidence boosts ability. What we lack in ability is made up through confidence. Let your confidence show when you pray. The Bible tells us that we should be and can be confident.

> *Therefore, brothers, since we have confidence... let us draw near to God...*

In every area of your life, at work, at school, at college, your business, your home, wherever - be confident.

Have confidence in Christ's wonderful saving act. Have confidence in yourself. God has confidence in you. God believes in you.

Confidence in a key to success. Confidence opens doors on earth. Be bold, because the Lord is with you.

You are a Key

Barnabas opened doors for Paul. Barnabas means 'son of encouragement'. Although Paul was dramatically converted, the early church still did not trust him. After all, Paul had persecuted them.

This is what happened when Paul tried to be accepted by the church in Jerusalem:

> *When he came to Jerusalem, he tried to join the disciples, but they were all afraid of him, not believing that he really was a disciple. But Barnabas took him and bought him and took him to the apostles. He told them how Saul on his journey had seen the Lord and that the Lord had spoken to him, and how in Damascus he had preached fearlessly in the name of Jesus* (Acts 9:26-27).

Barnabas took Paul to the apostles and explained his conversion experience and that he was now preaching Jesus as the Christ, the Son of God. They knew and respected Barnabas and believed what he said of Paul, and therefore accepted Paul as well. Barnabas was the key who opened the door for Paul.

Doors have opened for me through the Lord's people. Doors into Africa and Europe have been opened through those who knew me. Dozens of doors, for work in Britain and overseas, have been opened for me by my friend J. John. Korky Davey has opened doors for me in Greece and Nigeria.

You and I are keys that can open doors of blessing and opportunity for others. Be a blessing and open doors for others. Opening doors can be exciting. Opening doors can be ordinary.

You may not be able to do a certain thing, but you can cause someone else to do it. You may not be able to go and preach overseas, but you can give a financial gift to help someone else go instead. In return for opening doors for others you will receive the Lord's joy.

You are a key to opening doors. Obedience and confidence are also keys to opening doors.

Never, never belittle yourself, or what you can accomplish. If we can do big things let us do them, but we can all do little things. Let us do the little things well. Remember that there is value in little things.

> If I cannot do great things, I can do small things in a great way (J. F. Clarke). [2]

For 37 years Elezard Bouffier did something small each year:

> Over 10,000 people in Provence, France, owe their homes and environment to a little known peasant shepherd. Elezard Bouffier lived alone, in 1910, in a barren region where there were very few trees. While tending his flock in the Autumn, the shepherd would pick up each acorn that he saw. In the early Spring, while watching the sheep, he would prod the earth with his staff and drop in a nut. He did this each year between 1910 and 1947. At his death, the barren countryside was covered by trees and teaming with wild life. It is now the pleasant site of a new housing development. [3]

So plant your acorns today!

Chapter 12

Love Is ...

Mother Teresa of Calcutta died in the summer of 1997. There have been few people who have demonstrated such care and love towards the poor, neglected and dying. It was her belief in Christ's command to love our neighbour that enabled her to love the way she did. Mother Teresa's character was magnificent. The dictionary defines character as the collective qualities (especially mental and moral) that distinguish a person or thing.

Early on in her life she shared a story:

> Yes, the first woman I saw, I myself picked up from the street. She had been half eaten by rats and ants. I took her to the hospital but they could not do anything for her. They only took her in because I refused to move until they accepted her. From there, I went to the municipality and I asked them to give me a place where I could bring these people, because on the same day I had found other people dying in the streets. The health officer of the municipality took me to the temple, the Kali Temple, and showed me the *dormashalah* where the people used to rest after they had done their worship of the Kali goddess. It was an empty building; he asked me if I would accept it. I was very happy to have that place for many reasons, but especially knowing that it was a centre of devotion and worship of the Hindus. Within 24-hours, we had our patients there and we started the work of the home for the sick and dying who are destitute. Since then, we have picked up over 23,000 people from the streets of Calcutta of which 50 per cent have died. [1]

The loving character of Jesus is shown by Mark, the first century gospel writer. Jesus was characterised by love that knew no limits. What was he like? What kind of love was it? Jesus was patient and kind. He was not jealous or conceited or proud. He was not ill mannered, selfish or irritable. Jesus did not keep a record of wrongs. He was not happy with evil but was happy with the truth. Jesus never gave up. He had faith, hope and love for others, God and himself.

Love Calls

As Jesus walked along the seashore of Lake Galilee he saw two fishermen. They were Simon and his brother Andrew. They were busy catching fish with a net.

> 'Come follow me,' Jesus said, 'and I will make you fishers of men.'

Immediately the two brothers left their nets and went with Jesus. Love calls, believes, and makes you into someone different and better. Jesus called the first disciples to become fishers of men (Mark 1:16-18).

Love meets the Deepest Needs

The house where Jesus was teaching was full of people. The crowd overflowed outside. The paralysed man was lowered down through the roof in front of Jesus. Everyone could see the man's problem. It was obvious that he was paralysed. However the man had a deeper need. It was for forgiveness. Jesus said to him:

> 'Son, your sins are forgiven.' (Mark 12:1-12)

Then he healed him. Jesus meets the deepest needs. Jesus forgives.

Love Appoints and Sets Free

Jesus went up a mountain and called to himself those he wanted. The twelve disciples came to him. Jesus appointed and designated them apostles. They would be with him and he would send them out to preach. Jesus gave them the authority to drive out demons (Mark 3:13-19). Love appoints, and sets free to do good to others. Jesus appointed and designated apostles.

Love Calms a Storm

Jesus got into a boat with his disciples. Suddenly a furious, violent wind arose. The waves began to flood the boat. Jesus was at the back of the boat sleeping with his head on a pillow. His disciples woke him. They asked him if he cared that they were about to die. Jesus got up and spoke to the wind and the waves, commanding them to be still. The wind died down. There was a great calm. Love calms a storm. Jesus saved the disciples from drowning (Mark 4:35-41)

Love Heals

The incident where Jesus raises to life the daughter of Jairus and heals the sick woman is perhaps one of the most moving and loving gospel stories.

A synagogue ruler by the name of Jairus approached Jesus with faith and respect. He asked Jesus to save his dying daughter. Jairus falls to his feet and pleaded earnestly with Jesus:

> '*My little daughter is dying. Please come and put your hands on her so that she will be healed and live.*'

Jesus went with Jairus. On the way Jesus was confronted by a woman who had suffered from bleeding for twelve years. She touched Jesus' garment and is immediately healed. Jesus stops to affirm and confirm her faith publicly.

He continues his journey to Jairus' home only to find that the girl has died. This was not a problem. Jesus raised her to life. The girl stood up and walked around. She was just twelve years old. Everyone was amazed. Love heals. Jesus healed the daughter of Jairus and the sick woman (Mark 5:21-43).

Love Provides

Jesus was faced with a large crowd of hungry people. His disciples wanted to send them away to buy some food. Jesus was not impressed with this suggestion and intervened. Taking a few loaves and fish, he prayed to his Father. The food miraculously multiplied. The five thousand men plus women and children were fed. Love provides. Jesus fed the hungry. To the disciples he said:

> 'Give them something to eat yourselves.' (Matthew 14:16)

> Christians alone straddle the whole spectrum of rich nations and therefore Christians can be a lobby of tremendous importance. When we come before our heavenly Father and he says, 'Did you feed them, did you give them something to drink, did you clothe them, did you shelter them?' and we say, 'Sorry, Lord, but we did give them 0.3 per cent of our gross national product.' I don't think that will be enough.' (Barbara Ward) [2]

> Your poverty is greater than ours ... the spiritual poverty of the West is much greater than the physical poverty of the East. In the West, there are millions of people who suffer loneliness and emptiness, who feel unloved and unwanted. They are not the hungry in the physical sense; what is missing is a relationship with God and each other. (Mother Teresa) [3]

Love Listens to the Truth and Adjusts

Jesus went to the territory near to the city of Tyre where he went into a house. A Greek woman came and begged Jesus to deliver her daughter from evil (Mark 7:24-30):

> 'First let the children eat all they want,' he told her, 'for it is not right to take the children's bread and toss it to the dogs.'

In other words he said, 'No.' But the woman did not give up:

> *'Yes Lord,' she replied, 'but even the dogs under the table eat the children's crumbs.'*

Jesus listened and replied:

> *'For such a reply you may go; the demon has left your daughter.'*

Love listens to the truth and adjusts. Jesus listened to the woman and changed his mind. On returning home the Greek woman found her daughter well and the demon gone.

Love Rebukes

The disciples, especially Peter, got it wrong often. Peter did not approve when Jesus spoke to him of the suffering, rejection and death he was soon to encounter (Mark 8:31-33). Peter took Jesus aside and told him off for saying these things. Jesus turned and looked at his disciple and rebuked him:

> *'Get behind me, Satan!' he said. 'You do not have in mind the things of God, but the things of men.'*

Love rebukes. Jesus rebuked Peter.

Love Destroys the Work of Satan

A man brought his son to Jesus asking him for help (Mark 9:17-27). The boy could not hear or speak. Often his life was in danger because he would fall into water or fire. Jesus commanded the evil spirits that had hindered the boy's well-being to come out of him and never to enter him again. The boy shook. Jesus took him by the hand and he stood up. He was well. Love destroys the work of Satan. Jesus delivered a boy from evil spirits. The Son of God appeared for this very reason, to destroy the work of the Devil (1 John 3:8).

Love Welcomes All

People brought children to Jesus for him to place his hands on them and to bless them (Mark 10:13-16). The disciples wrongly rebuked the people. When Jesus saw this he was angry and rebuked his disciples saying,

> *'Let the little children come to me, and do not hinder them, for the kingdom of God belongs to such as these.'*

Jesus welcomed these children. He took them in his arms and placed his hands on each of them, blessing them again and again. Love welcomes all. Jesus welcomes all people, whatever age, colour or background.

Love Demonstrates Righteous Indignation

On reaching Jerusalem Jesus came to the temple area (Mark 11:12-19). This area was the only part of the temple in which the Gentiles could worship God and gather for prayer. The area, that was reserved for Gentiles, was occupied with tables, money changers and animal pens. The court of the Gentiles became a noisy, smelly market place. The Jewish religious leaders were interfering with the provision that God had given to the Gentiles. Jesus made a whip out of cords (John 2:15) and used it to drive all from that place, including sheep and cattle. He overturned the tables of the money changers, scattering coins everywhere. He allowed no one to carry any goods through. 'Stop!' Jesus told the people:

> *'My temple will be called a house of prayer for all nations. But you have made it "a den of robbers".'*

The whole crowd was amazed at his teaching. The chief Priests and teachers of the law were afraid of him and began looking for ways to kill him.

They knew he was absolutely right. Jesus knew that his action would infuriate them. He was not afraid of their feelings because he was at home with his own feelings. Jesus is more often thought of in terms of his compassion, gentleness and restraint; but he also knew the whole range of emotions, some of them very passionate and disturbing. Jesus' response to the injustice in the temple was righteous.

In his book *Anger - What to do about it* Richard Walters writes:

> Indignation is the proper reaction to injustice if it energises our physical and emotional systems to oppose evil, to right the wrongs that have been done to those we care about, and to work hard for social changes that will spare others from abuse and suffering. Feelings of anger can spring out of a Christian's sensitivity to human welfare. While rage and resentment are aggressive, seeking to destroy their target, indignation seeks to mobilise the forces of good to challenge and defeat the forces of destruction and oppression.

Love demonstrates righteous indignation or anger. Jesus cleared the temple displaying his anger and brought justice; that was love.

Love Has Integrity

Some Pharisees and Herodians came to Jesus commenting on his moral excellence:

> '*Teacher, we know you are a man of integrity. You are not swayed by men, because you pay no attention to who they are; but you teach the way of God in accordance with the truth.*' (Mark 12:13-14)

They were correct even though they had a hidden agenda and wanted to catch him out. Jesus had integrity. He was honest, sound, right, transparent; what you saw of him in public, was true in private. Love has integrity. Jesus demonstrated this quality throughout his life.

The founder of the Salvation Army, General William Booth,

cared for the hungry and the poor. He advanced the Christian faith through the preaching of the good news of Jesus Christ. He and his non-violent army fought for justice. He said:

> While women weep as they do now, I'll fight; while little children go hungry as they do now, I'll fight; while men go to prison, in and out, I'll fight; while there is a poor lost girl upon the street, I'll fight; while there yet remains one dark soul without the light of God, I'll fight - I'll fight to the very end. [4]

Love Foresees, Warns and Says be Careful

Sitting on the Mount of Olives, opposite the temple, Jesus spoke to Peter, James, John and Andrew about the future (Mark 13:5-12,23). He foresaw what will happen concerning the world. He spoke to them about wars, nations fighting one another, earth-quakes multiplying, and future famines. Jesus told them what will happen to them personally. He warned them and told them to watch their step. Love foresees, warns and says be careful.

David Wilkerson, the American Evangelist, one day foresaw something in the life of the evangelist, Jimmy Swaggett. Wilkerson told Swaggatt to separate himself and to be careful. Unfortunately Swaggatt did not listen to the warning and was not careful. Swaggatt committed adultery with a prostitute. Although these events occurred in America the news appeared on national British television. Television news showed Jimmy Swaggett apologising for his behaviour. I am afraid it was too late. He would have to live with the consequences. Jesus warns and says be careful. Allow his spirit to speak to you about your life. Allow his spirit to speak through you to others.

Love Sacrifices

In the garden of Gethsemane on Thursday evening, a few hours before that horrific crucifixion, Jesus experienced physical and mental torture. He was arrested by the religious leaders, severely beaten and spat on. Jesus became a sacrifice to save humanity.

Love sacrifices. Jesus in the garden was almost overwhelmed to the point of death (Mark 14:13-21). This is sacrificial love.

> The story is told by the Persians of the great Shah Abbas, who reigned magnificently in Persia, but loved to mingle with the people in disguise. Once, dressed as a poor man, he descended the long flight of stairs, dark and damp, to the tiny cellar where the fireman, seated on ashes, was tending the furnace.
>
> The king sat down beside him and began to talk. At meal time the fireman produced some coarse, black bread and a jug of water and they ate and drank. The Shah went away, but returned again and again, for his heart was filled with sympathy for the lonely man. He gave him sweet counsel, and the poor man opened his whole heart and loved this friend, so kind, so wise, and yet poor like himself.
>
> At last the emperor thought, 'I will tell him who I am, and see what gift he will ask.' So he said, 'You think me poor, but I am Shah Abbas your emperor.' He expected a petition for some great thing, but the man sat silent, gazing on him with love and wonder. Then the king said, 'Haven't you understood? I can make you rich and noble, can give you a city, can appoint you a great ruler. Have you nothing to ask?'
>
> The man replied gently, 'Yes, my lord, I understood. But what is this you have done, to leave your palace and glory, to sit with me in this dark place, to partake of my coarse fare, to care whether my heart is glad or sorry? Even you can give nothing more precious. On others you may bestow rich presents, but to me you have given yourself; it only remains to ask that you never withdraw this gift of your friendship.' [5]

Love is Willing to Die

The greatest demonstration of love is for a person to give their life for another. Jesus said:

'Greater love has no one than this, that he lay down his life for his friends.' (John 15:13)

Jesus allowed himself to be arrested, flogged and crucified because of his great love for humanity (Mark 15). His death and shed blood brings forgiveness and new life today for all who repent, believe and receive new birth by the Holy Spirit. Jesus' death proved and showed his love for us. Love is willing to die. Jesus was crucified. Here is love, vast as the ocean.

Love Wins

Love never fails. In the end love will win through. Having killed Jesus they thought that would be the end of him. Death could not hold Jesus. Jesus rose again (Mark 16:1-8). Love wins through. Jesus is risen.

Chapter 13

Marriage

One of the most neglected subjects in church life is that of marriage. But a high percentage of those who attend church are married or plan to marry one day. Whether married or single, relationships are what life is about.

One day I asked my congregation, which consisted of all ages, married and single people, to write down what was their deepest need. The most common answer by far was 'to be loved' or 'love'.

In my work in this country and overseas I have discovered that whenever I speak on marriage matters, love or sex, I get the most response. People come to speak to me afterwards, others want advice; some are experiencing difficulties in their marriage, and some are in tears.

Once I gave a brief book review at a Youth Celebration packed with teenagers. I read out the chapter headings from the book by J. John *It's Always On My Mind*;

- For Love's Sake
- Love Yourself
- Guilty Chains ... Broken Boundaries
- The Pains and Pleasures of Growing Up
- Going Out
- Why Wait Till Marriage for Sex?
- How Far Do You Go?
- Single and Waiting
- Finding a Partner - How Do I Know?
- Loneliness

I had 100 copies of the book, still wrapped in plastic, with me. Every single copy was sold. People want to know about love, sex and marriage, because they want to better their relationships.

Those people with good marriages can have great marriages. For those who have settled for a mediocre marriage - it does not have to be that way. For those people who are struggling in marriage - things can change, do not give up.

Close to the end of his life Winston Churchill was asked to give a speech at Harrow School in England. One of the greatest men in British history made his way slowly to the podium. Churchill's speech lasted less than one minute, but it drew a standing ovation. What did he say? With his unforgettable, deep, gruff voice he said:

> Never give up... Never, never give up... Never, never, never give up. [1]

What he said has encouraged men and women ever since.

The foundational aspects of marriage are that of leaving, cleaving and being united with your partner. The other necessary qualities and aspects of marriage are built upon these foundations.

The first foundation of marriage is leaving.

> *For this cause a man will leave his father and mother and will be united to his wife, and they will become one flesh* (Genesis 2:24).

The man and woman leave their parents and become detached from them. There cannot be cleaving without leaving. A physical and emotional severance is needed. For the married couple it means that their first dedication and commitment is to each other and no longer to their parents. It means that the newly married couples' first love now goes to their spouse and not to parents. The direction of their relationship changes from parents to spouse. This will have consequences forever. If either of the married couple has to choose between spouse and parent, they should, unquestioningly, choose spouse. This is not being cruel but a matter of priority. However parents should continue to be honoured. Biblical marriage demands a change in priorities. Few marriages will survive without leaving, where the 'umbilical cord' with parents is not severed.

In marriage the man and the woman cleave to each other. They are united. The essence of marriage is the exclusiveness of it. No one and nothing should be allowed to disturb the wonderful, exclusive union between man and woman. Professor Tasker has written concerning married persons:

> Who felt no jealousy, at the intrusion of a lover or an adulterer into their home, would surely be lacking in moral perception, for the exclusiveness of the marriage is the essence of marriage. [2]

The man and woman leave all, cleave together and become one flesh. It is only in marriage that one plus one equals one. You have become one with your spouse. A husband and wife uniquely blend together without losing their individual identities. A union takes place but the individuality is not removed only refined. This union means that little can affect one without affecting the other. It means caring for your partner as you care for yourself. It also means learning how to anticipate his or her needs and helping the other person to become all they can be. We retain our character and identity as man and woman but one plus one always equals one in marriage.

Love and Respect

In Paul's letter, there are three times as many words telling husbands to love their wives as there are words telling wives to submit to their husbands (Compare Ephesians 5:25-33 and Ephesians 5:22-24). Paul says:

> *Husbands love your wives ...*

Paul was probably married at one time. We know that this is probable because to have been a member of the Sanhedrin, as Paul was, there was a requirement to be married.

What kind of love does a man have for his wife? First it is a sacrificial love.

> *Husbands love your wives, just as Christ loved the Church and gave himself up for her* (Ephesians 5:25).

When a husband loves his wife enough to die for her, he is loving her in the same way as Christ loved the Church. Sacrificial love goes to the limit, pays the price, suffers loss, endures being inconvenienced and undergoes pain. Sacrificial love has no conditions even to the point of death.

A husband loves his wife with the kind of love that makes her holy and clean. Paul says:

> *...to make her holy, cleansing her ...* (Ephesians 5:26)

It is love that refines the character. Love is the great purifier of life. A husband has responsibility to take his wife and himself deeper into God's holiness. To do this he needs to set an example and to be a role model in holiness.

Recently I invited my wife, Annette, to a conference for evangelists because I wanted her to benefit from hearing the teaching and experience the times of worship. It is important for couples to continue developing in Christian character and for them to grow together in their walk with God. It is easy for one of the couple to be lagging behind the other in their passion for Christ and his purposes. It is easy for the couple to grow apart.

A loving husband nourishes his wife

> *After all no one ever hated his own body, but he feeds and cares for it, just as Christ does the church* (Ephesians 5:29).

A husband can keep his wife properly nourished by feeding her physically and spiritually, by helping her into a deeper understanding of God's Word.

A husband's love should be a love that cares. Everyone cares for his own body; we look after ourselves. Husbands should care for their wives as they care for their own bodies. Our wives should matter to us; they are important and essential.

Love respects another. Husbands are called to treat their wives with respect.

> *Husbands, in the same way be considerate as you live with your wives, and treat them with respect as the weaker partner and as heirs with you of the gracious gift of life, so that nothing will hinder your prayers* (1 Peter 3:7).

Husbands are to be considerate as they live with their wives. Some men treat those they employ with more respect than their wives. Respect means to think well of and hold in high regard. It means making sure you notice her. Respect is appreciating and admiring.

There is a specific word to wives concerning respecting their husbands (Ephesians 5:33).

It is the husband's responsibility to love his wife as Christ loved the church. One word of warning. Nowhere in the Bible is a wife commanded to get her husband to love her properly. Another warning. Nowhere in the Bible is the husband commanded to demand his wife be properly submissive to him. The Word of God does say that each husband and wife is to focus on their own responsibility.

Submit

We are taught:

> *Submit to one another out of reverence for Christ* (Ephesians 5:21).

Christ submitted his will to that of his heavenly Father. We honour Jesus by following his example and by also submitting to God. To submit means to cease resistance or surrender our will to another. Although there is a mutual submitting to each other, between man and woman; there is a distinct and different submission that a wife gives to her husband:

> *Wives, submit to your husbands as to the Lord. For the husband is the head of the wife as Christ is the head of the church* (Ephesians 5:22-24).

Submission is often misunderstood. It does not mean becoming a door mat. In a marriage the wife is called to submit to her husband. For the wife, it means to freely follow her husband's leadership in Christ. For the husband, it means putting aside his own interests in order to care for his wife.

The Apostle Paul taught believers to submit to one another by choice (Ephesians 5:21). Mutual submission preserves order and harmony in the family while it increases love and respect amongst family members. The Bible says that the man is the spiritual head of the family. This means that his wife should acknowledge his leadership. His leadership involves service; just as Christ served his disciples so the husband is to serve his wife. A husband should not abuse or take advantage of his position of leadership. A wife should not try to undermine her husband's leadership. Either of these wrong attitudes would cause friction in a marriage.

Communication

Meaningful communication and conversation is essential in marriage. It has been my observation that this is especially appreciated by wives. It is true that some men do not value this as highly as their wives.

Meaningful communication and conversation between husband and wife is an important aspect of a successful marriage. For this to happen adequate time must be created. Many people's lives are too busy. We tend to live to the maximum. Some people have demanding jobs that sap their time and energy. The problem can be that when a husband and wife do come together, they are too tired or unable to switch off. Something somewhere is wrong. It is good to talk. We can only meet each other's needs if we communicate and know what they really are, not what we think they are.

Men and woman have different needs. From time to time our needs change. We need to talk and communicate our needs to each other. Proper communication, including talking, is healthy.

Project

Look at the two lists below. Using 1 to 11, write down the order in which they are of importance to you as a husband or wife. Once you have completed this, share your list with your partner. This could help you to meet each others needs, with the increased understanding that comes through communicating the needs that are important to you both.

As a Wife: My Needs in Marriage Are:	
	Affection
	Sex
	Conversation
	Recreational Time Together
	Financial Support
	Attractiveness of my Husband
	Honesty and Openness
	Domestic Support
	Family Commitment
	Admiration
	Love

As a Husband: My Needs in Marriage Are:	
	Affection
	Sex
	Conversation
	Recreational Time Together
	Financial Support
	Attractiveness of my Wife
	Honesty and Openness
	Domestic Support
	Family Commitment
	Admiration
	Love

Making Love

The following letters appeared in the *Daily Telegraph* in October 1997. They were addressed to Aunt Anne Atkins.

My husband won't touch me

Dear Anne - I have been married for nine years and love my husband very much, but his behaviour makes me so unhappy that I am wondering whether I should get a divorce. For the past few years, he has refused to hug, kiss or make love to me. If I touch him, even accidentally, he flinches and moves away. No amount of talking, crying or shouting makes any difference to him: he simply walks away, or shuts his eyes and pretends to be asleep. He does not even want to spend time with our eight-year-old daughter, and seems much more interested in his computing job than in his family. Should I leave him? I desperately want my girl to have a father at home, but I can't cope with the thought of spending the rest of my life in such loneliness.

Your husband must be made to see that his behaviour is unfair. Instead of crying or shouting, try to find his Achilles heel. One wife I know told her (very eminent) husband that if he hit again, she would tell their vicar: he mended his ways immediately. Another friend got so fed up with her husband, who persistently worked late, that she threatened to throw his £8,000 computer out of the window. In the end she locked him out of the house and said she would send his suitcase on to his office. He now comes home on time.

Stay calm, but tell him you are thinking of giving his beloved computer to the church jumble. Or take his car keys so that he has to walk to work. Whatever it takes to make him treat your feelings with respect. Remind him that your marriage is worth far more to you than his job or car or anything else.

Then when he agrees to your terms, insist on a weekly session with a Relate counsellor for an initial minimum of six months to a year.

On no account whatsoever should you leave your house. Your husband is at fault, not you.

————————

Dear Anne - I strongly disagree with your views on 'conjugal rights'. Sex in marriage is not a right, but a privilege. Only a cad would insist on such 'rights'. Nor do I agree with your proposition that, as long as the couple concerned is legally married, 'anything goes' as far as sex is concerned. To judge from some of your replies, you seem to think that a woman should behave like a nun before the wedding, and like a prostitute afterwards!

————————

Yes, I think that sums up the Christian attitude to sex pretty neatly. I agree that only a cad would demand these rights in an unloving way; but only a cad would deny them, too.

St. Paul said that a married person has no authority over his body; he owes it to his spouse to make love frequently (1 Corinthians 7:4). Which just goes to show that obedience to God can be jolly good fun.

In 1 Corinthians 7:2-5, Paul gives instructions concerning the sexual aspect in marriage. Why is it that there are Christian couples who have thrown out the sexual aspect of their marriage? Perhaps they think it is optional. We understand that there can be genuine reasons why a couple do not or very seldom make love within their marriage.

One valued reason is that one (or both) of them are prevented from doing so because of a disease or illness. Another reason may be that both of them have communicated properly about their feelings and desires and each of them are happy to abstain from sexual activity. These are good and valued reasons, however all is not well when there is no physical reason and one of the couple would prefer to have sex. The Bible teaches:

> *But since there is so much immorality, each man should*
> *have his own wife, and each woman her own husband.*
> *The husband should fulfil his marital duty to his wife,*
> *and likewise the wife to her husband. The wife's body*
> *does not belong to her alone but also to her husband. In*
> *the same way, the husband's body does not belong to him*
> *alone but also to his wife. Do not deprive each other*
> *except by mutual consent and for a time, so that you may*
> *devote yourselves to prayer. Then come together again so*
> *that Satan will not tempt you because of your lack of self-*
> *control. I say this as a concession, not as a command. I*
> *wish that all men were as I am. But each man has his own*
> *gift from God; one has this gift, another has that* (1
> Corinthians 7:2-5).

I say again unless that you have a physical reason or that you
have consented to abstain from sex, then there is a problem.

As married people we have no rights to our bodies, as Joyce
Huggett points out:

> Cynthia seemed to believe that since sex for her was a
> non-event, she had every right to make it difficult for Ron
> to make love to her. This is not correct. When we marry,
> we forfeit our rights, even to our own body. The Bible
> emphasises that married couples should not defraud one
> another sexually unless they do so for an agreed, limited,
> period, and for the sake of prayer. Failure to obey this
> biblical injunction results in intolerable pain for at least
> one partner: the pain of rejection. This pain gives birth to
> a disharmony that percolates through to the entire rela-
> tionship.[3]

The husband and wife fulfil their duty to give themselves to
each other because their bodies belong to their partner. By keep-
ing your body to yourself, you are being selfish. In making love
you are giving pleasure to your husband or wife. Those who are
married are told not to deprive each other sexually. The partner
who is deprived is very unhappy. Some of the most miserable

people I have met are those who are deprived of sex by their partners. It is no surprise, therefore, that Christians have secret affairs. Happy, healthy, sexual relations are vital to marriage.

A husband wrote this letter to his wife:

To my ever-loving wife,

During the past year, I have attempted to seduce you 365 times. I succeeded 36 times. This averages once every ten days. The following is a list of excuses made on unsuccessful occasions:

We will wake		Not in the mood	21
the children	7	The baby is crying	18
It's too hot	15	Watched late	
It's too cold	3	night show	7
Too tired	19	Watched early show	15
It's too early	9	Mudpack on	12
It's too late	16	Grease on face	6
Pretending to sleep	33	Reading Sunday paper	10
Windows open		We have company	
- neighbours will hear	3	in the next room	7
Your back ached	16	Your parents were	
Toothache	2	staying with us	5
Headache	26	My parents were	
Giggling fit	2	staying with us	5
I've had too		Is that all you ever	
much to drink	4	think about	105

Do you think you could improve our record this coming year?
Your ever-loving husband [4]

Joyce Huggett, in her book on conflict, says this in her chapter on 'Sex - A Subtle Weapon',

Stories of sex indifference in marriage, of monotonous

sex, mediocre sex, or withholding could fill several pages. They are a common phenomena in marriage. This is serious because the difference between a marriage where sex is mutually satisfying and marriage where one or both partners fail to find sexual fulfilment is the difference between a sun-splashed day in spring and a drab, grey-wet November day. Whether we like to admit it or not, sex in marriage colours everything.[5]

Sex cannot be kept apart from other aspects of marriage. Joyce Huggett writes:

Sex colours everything. The reverse is also true. Everything else colours sex. Thus a couple who have been working too hard, depriving one another of companionship, communication, tenderness or sensitivity are unlikely to enjoy mutually satisfying sex. Similarly, a couple who have become neglectful of personal hygiene... the couple whose night attire has become shabby, might find this drabness and self-neglect reflected in their love-making. These factors may not give rise to brawls or open conflict. They may accumulate and contribute to the conglomeration of marital disharmony of which sexual non-relating is one part. [6]

Sex is best when you take your time. Love-making in marriage joins the couple together in oneness. It is an unspoken language. Doctors tell us that sex is good for our health. Good sexual relations will bring completion, enjoyment and healing. One of the many myths about sex is that both partners should be in the mood. Another myth is that the husband should always take the initiative in sexual activity. Couples need to find a time and position and a technique that is comfortable, relaxing and exciting to them.

Chapter 14
Natural Evangelism

Natural evangelism is sharing the good news of Jesus in an easy manner, with no artificial ingredients. About 80 percent of those who become Christians do so because of friendship with a follower of Christ. Friendship evangelism is the most fruitful and effective form of sharing the Good News. Evangelism done through friendship is not as daunting as some people think. With God's help you can successfully share the Good News with your friends.

Why Evangelise?

The most important reason why we should evangelise is because Jesus told us to do so. Jesus spoke to his disciples and gave them the great commission:

> 'All authority in heaven and on earth has been given to me. Therefore go and make disciples of all nations, baptising them in the name of the Father and of the Son and of the Holy Spirit, and teaching them to obey everything I have commanded you. And surely I am with you always, to the very end of the age.' (Matthew 28:18-20)

The Church is unique in that it exists for its non-members. Neil Rowe of the Worldwide Evangelisation Crusade has said:

> We as Christians, have done a thousand and one things Jesus never commanded us to do, but we have failed in the two 'new' commandments that he gave to the Church. We have failed to love one another and we have failed to preach the gospel to every nation.

Christ's commandment to share the gospel is important, but somehow the important is replaced by the urgency of everyday living.

The second reason why we should evangelise is that people without Christ are missing out. They may not realise they are missing out, but nevertheless they are. Christ gives peace; a peace that the world cannot give or understand. Jesus offers forgiveness from the past. He breaks the power of sin. He sets us free from our prisons.

Being a Christian means knowing God and Jesus personally. Jesus offers the assurance of eternal life. To the repentant thief on the cross Jesus promised:

> 'You shall be with me in Paradise.' (Luke 23:43)

We read that as Jesus saw the crowds, he felt a great compassion for them because they were harassed and helpless like sheep without a shepherd (Matthew 9:36). Those without Christ miss out on the wonderful blessings that we have mentioned. They have no one to look after them and their needs. They are journeying through life without reaching great possibilities with Jesus. Out of compassion let us begin to cultivate our friendships with non-believers. They need the Saviour of the world. Jesus is the good shepherd who cares for lost sheep.

Paul wanted Philemon, a believer in Colossae and a slave owner, to know the consequences of sharing the faith. Paul wrote to him:

> I pray that you may be active in sharing your faith so that you will have a fuller understanding of every good thing we have in Christ. (Philemon:6)

Those who share their faith experience a deeper understanding of what they have in Christ.

Another reason why we evangelise is because it is fun! One day I got the train at Liverpool Street Station in London. As I entered the carriage I observed that there was only one other passenger. He was a young oriental man. I sat opposite him. I wanted to share something of Jesus with him, but I could not open my mouth. I prayed:

Lord, for some reason I cannot start a conversation and I do so want to speak to him. I ask you Lord to open his mouth and make him ask me what book I am holding in my hand. If you do that I will take it up from there. Amen.

The man immediately spoke up and asked me what book I was holding. I told it was my New Testament and briefly shared something about Christianity. He seemed open. I gave him my New Testament and excused myself as I was way past my stop. I prayed for that man. It was fun.

There are different definitions of evangelism. A correct and healthy definition of biblical evangelism is necessary, otherwise we will become discouraged. Jesus said:

> *'Go into all the world and preach the good news to all creation. Whoever believes and is baptised will be saved, but whoever does not believe will be condemned.'* (Mark 16:15-16)

Notice that our task is just this - go preach the good news. We have discharged our responsibility when the message has been shared. Those who hear it have a choice to either follow Christ or not. What they do with the message of life is between them and God. Those who decide to obey Christ, the Church disciples and looks after (Matthew 28:19-20). They are received into the Church (Acts 2:37-47).

> *On one occasion Jesus sent out the twelve disciples with the following instructions, 'As you go preach this message: "The kingdom of heaven is near"... If anyone will not welcome you or listen to your words, shake the dust off your feet when you leave that home of town.'* (Matthew 10:7,14)

Move on if the message is rejected. If the message is received, there will be nurturing and follow-up to be done.

Friendship Evangelism

Our church organised a mission with a visiting evangelist. We had arranged two of the meetings to be held in a restaurant in the city. The plan was to invite guests for a three course meal and to hear the after-dinner speaker who would speak about life and Christ. The guests were paid for by church members or from the evangelism account.

Prior to the meeting my friend Eric Harmer had done some excellent door to door visitation. The response from people was most encouraging. Eric brought two couples to my attention. As he was unable to visit them again he asked me to visit them and invite them to the dinner meeting. Sarah, a member of the church, and I visited these couples and invited them to the meal. Both couples accepted gladly.

They came along and sat with my wife and I throughout the evening. When the speaker had finished his gospel address, he had a brief prayer for anyone who wanted to become a Christian. Coffee was then served and people began chatting.

I asked Joyce what she thought of the evening. She told me that she had accepted Jesus as her saviour that very evening, during the prayer. Although Joyce had gone to church and had believed in Jesus, she was not a Christian. She did not know the necessity of being born again. She began to attend the church and its discipleship group. In a very short space of time Joyce had come to Christ through four Christians who visited her in her home and then inviting her to an event. That is friendship evangelism.

George and Lily were the other couple Eric asked us to visit. They both received Jesus as their saviour on that evening. As I leaned over to ask Lily how she was feeling, she explained that she was not baptised and was concerned. Soon she was baptised at the age of 71. She also continued to follow Christ and attend church.

Francis is a hairdresser. Every time I needed my hair cut I would go to the place where he worked. Six or more times a year for seven years Francis cut my hair. He would often open up to me and tell me about his life. I wanted him to come and hear me preach the good news at a guest service. I knew that although we knew each other the bridge between us was not strong enough for him to accept the invitation to come to church. I had a good thought. I would invite him for a meal at lunch time. I picked him up from work and we went to the local Chinese restaurant. On the way back I invited him to the guest service and gave him an invitation card. Francis had not been inside a church for a very long time. He accepted the card and came and heard the gospel.

In friendship evangelism we are building bridges with people. There has to be a degree of respect and trust before they will receive the message.

Natural evangelism is not difficult. Over a period of two years I had gotten to know the manager of a local Indian restaurant. Every time I went in he was always friendly and pleasant towards me. Without realising it, I was bridge building with him over that time. I invited him to a restaurant meeting. He came. He heard the gospel. He said to me after the address that he was contemplating the Christian faith as alternative to Islam.

I invited Peter and Margaret, Jan and Lucy, Fred and Beryl to a gospel event in a restaurant. They all came. That evening they all heard the simple offer of salvation and they had an enjoyable evening. Why did they come? At the time they were our neighbours and we had known them for several years. I prayed that they would come. Natural evangelism is about spending time with friends.

At the moment I building a bridge with an insurance man. I have known him for eight years. I am still building a bridge. I pray and hope that one day he will accept an invitation to a suitable event to hear the gospel of Jesus.

Sharing Jesus Spontaneously

One day, on my flight back from Addis Ababa, Ethiopia, I noticed a young man sitting nearby. I had an urge to speak to him about Jesus. I took out a little gospel booklet called *Knowing God*. I leaned over to him and introduced myself. I gave him the booklet and he received it gladly. From the corner of my eye I could see him carefully reading it. After 20 minutes of reading he turned to me. Pointing to a paragraph in the booklet he said, 'What does it mean to be born again?' I began by sharing with him that he and I had something in common, that of our Orthodox backgrounds. I pointed out the difference between knowing about God and knowing God personally. I told him about Jesus and Nicodemus in John chapter 3 and of the necessity of being born again. We spoke for an hour. I gave him my address and told him I would pleased if he wrote to me.

The young woman behind the counter was uncertain if the work we had given her to do would come out well. I said that if the job came out well I would give her two free tickets to a restaurant meeting. A few days later I went back to pick up the posters. They were fine. I gave her the tickets and a few weeks later she came to the meeting with her brother Ken. During the evening Annette and I sat with them. We listened to the speaker afterwards and had an enjoyable evening.

A few weeks later Ken was reading the Bible in the bath! One verse in Matthew's gospel got his attention. There and then Ken made a decision to give his life to Christ. Shortly afterward his girlfriend Elizabeth also became a Christian. They were later married and have become dedicated followers of Jesus. Today Ken is doing a one year, full-time training course in evangelism.

One of my favourite ways of evangelism is giving a book or booklet to someone. For over twenty-three years I have given countless books to individuals. While on a University mission, I noticed a student looking at the book stall. I saw him pick up an excellent book by J. John called *Dead Sure?* He put it down. I quickly went over to him, introduced myself, and gave him a copy of the book as a gift from me. He took it gladly. The next day he came to the venue again. I asked him how he had gotten on with the book? He said that he had read it all, from cover to cover. Stephen did not just read the book; he read it with an open mind. He explained that he had committed his life to Jesus as the book had suggested. We had coffee together and chatted about what it means to follow Jesus. I found out later that Stephen went on to be baptised and attend church regularly.

We can all give a book. We may never know the outcome. It does not matter. We can all pray for those who do not know

Christ. We can give money to causes that advance the gospel. We can write a letter to a friend or relative.

Two years before my father died I wrote a letter to him. I thanked him and told him that I loved him. I encouraged him to read the enclosed evangelistic paper. I felt compelled to give him the gospel in the form of words printed on a page. What he did with it all, I will never know. We must do something. We can do something.

Growing in Confidence

The Gospel is powerful. The telling of it is powerful. The reading of it is powerful. When I speak the Gospel to individuals or at gatherings, whether they be large or small, I believe hearts will be touched because the Gospel is presented. There is an inherent power in the Gospel. Jesus died for our sins and rose again, and is able to impart his life and blessings, offering forgiveness of sins (1 Corinthians 15:3-7). God honours the preaching, sharing, chatting of the gospel. Paul wrote:

> *I am not ashamed of the gospel because it is the power of God for the salvation of everyone who believes* (Romans 1:16).

Put your faith in that statement. Put your trust in the gospel, not in your ability. God has always blessed the sharing of the gospel. Remember that Jesus promises to be with us:

> *'Surely I am with you always.'* (Matthew 28:20)

That is no idle promise. Let its truth grip your soul. You are not alone. You do not go in your own strength. Face your fears knowing he is with you and that he lives in you. God believes in you. Have confidence. Jesus said:

> *'You are the light of the world.'* (Matthew 5:14)

God has passed the baton on to us because he believes we can win the race and do the job, the job of sharing the message of life.

Jesus said:

> '... *apart from me you can do nothing.*' (John 15:5)

We depend on him for everything. We can do no good thing without Jesus. It is also true that Jesus will not do anything without us. Jesus depends on us. He has entrusted you and me with the most important thing in the world, to bring salvation of others. Jesus is surely with you. Let your confidence grow as these truths are imbedded in your soul. We have at our disposal God's ultimate resource, his Holy Spirit, to empower us for action.

Jesus told his church not to attempt evangelisation until they were empowered by the Holy Spirit (Luke 24:48-49). According to Jesus we need only ask the Holy Spirit, and he will fill us to over flowing (Luke 11:11-13).

The Holy Spirit is given to help us share our faith. It is not a task to be attempted on our own. That does not mean that we will not go in fear and trembling. At times Paul went with knees knocking (1 Corinthians 2:3-5).

The Local Church and Evangelism

The local church has the responsibility of reaching out to the community with the good news. It also has the responsibility for social action. There are four things that the local church can do to make evangelism work.

1   A church engaged or wanting to be engaged in successful evangelism needs to put on suitable events for its members to feel able to bring along their non Christian friends.

In my travels, both in this country and overseas, I have discovered that what works in one place may not work in another. Usually events that involve a social aspect and food work extremely well in Britain. Guests are happy to come to a neutral venue instead of church premises. Guests are happy to socialise, eat and drink. They do not feel threatened or embarrassed. The local church must consider this before it puts on an event. Certain questions need to be asked. Is this venue or event likely to encourage people to come along or not? How do the Christians feel about the event? If Christians have no confidence in the event or the speaker, it will not work. I have managed to bring along dozens of non Christians to events who would never have entered the door of a church.

The Church must make it easy for people to hear the Gospel, not difficult. The Church must go to people, not expect people to come to it.

2 The local church could regularly have a mini or full blown mission, lasting from two to seven days. In addition, certain times of the year, such as Christmas, provide great opportunities. Many churches have visitors who want to attend a Christmas service. In Britain more unchurched people will enter through the doors of a church at Christmas than at any other time of year. We should take advantage of this.

Proper preparation before the mission is vital to its fruitfulness. It is useful to have an evangelist from outside of the local church for missions. It is necessary for the evangelist to train the church and for the Christians to meet him and get to like him.

3 The local church needs to invest financially in local evangelism. It is sad that most churches are willing to allocate funds for various things in church life, but neglect to allow for an evangelism programme. Perhaps as a start ten percent or more of the income of the local church should be set aside for evangelism.

4 The local church must invest time, energy, and money in evangelism. The Sunday teaching programme should reflect from time to time the basics of Christianity. Subjects like 'Why evangelise?', 'How to share your faith', 'How to share your testimony', 'Who was Jesus?', 'Why did he die?', 'Heaven and hell', 'How to become a Christian', are all helpful to old and new Christians alike.

Remember the Church exists for its non-members. The salvation of souls must come first. Jesus said that the two most important commandments were to love God and our neighbour as ourselves. This involves sharing the Gospel and social action.

Chapter 15

Other Side

The disciples had been with Jesus for some time before this boat journey. They saw his first miracle at the wedding in Cana, Galilee (John 2:1-12). The wine had run out so Jesus changed 20 gallons of water into wine. It was the moment that the disciples put their faith in him.

On another occasion James and John went to Andrew and Simon Peter's home, where Simon Peter's mother-in-law was sick in bed with a fever. Jesus came and healed her. That same evening, after sunset, it seemed as if the whole town had gathered at the door of the house. Jesus healed many of various diseases. He drove out demons (Mark 1:29-34).

The disciples witnessed the healing of a man with a paralysed hand. This took place on the Sabbath (Mark 3:1-6). The disciples saw Jesus minister deliverance, healing and miracles. His teaching was amazing bringing hope and strength to all.

Jesus Promises

Now after all these events Jesus says to the disciples:

> *'Let us go to the other side.'* (Mark 4:35-41)

The boat journey across the Sea of Galilee was about 5 miles. Unknown to the disciples their faith in Christ's ability was going to be tested.

The crowd was left behind. Unexpectedly and without warning a strong wind blew up. The lake was notorious for its storms. Storms came out of the blue with terrifying consequences. Waves began to enter the boat until it was full of water. Jesus was sleeping at the back of the boat. The disciples woke him:

'Teacher, don't you care if we drown?'
He got up, rebuked the wind and said to the waves,
'Quiet! Be still!' Then the wind died down and it was
completely calm.

Once Jesus dealt with the immediate threat to the lives of his
beloved disciples, he asked them:

'Why are you so afraid? Do you still have no faith?'

They could not cope with all that had happened. They were
afraid and said to each other:

'Who is this? Even the wind and the waves obey him!'

At the outset of this journey Jesus promised the disciples that
they were going over to the other side. Jesus meant what he
said. He was not going to lose any of his friends on the way.
In the storm the disciples forgot Jesus' words and promise.
Perhaps they thought he was casually talking when he spoke
those words. However his promise was a sure thing. The
promise is as valuable as the fulfilment. When Christ speaks to
us we must believe and remember the words spoken.
Otherwise we can experience unnecessary difficulties. More
things happen when God talks to us, and we act on it, than
when we talk to God.

The Centurion sent his servants to Jesus telling him it was
not necessary for him to come to his house in person, but to
only say the word and his servant would be healed (Luke 7:7).
The Centurion knew that the words spoken by Christ held
power.

Once when Jesus was walking on the water, towards his disciples, they were afraid because they thought he was a ghost.

But Jesus immediately said to them: 'Take courage! It is
I. Don't be afraid.' 'Lord, if it's you,' Peter replied, 'tell
me to come to you on the water.'

Jesus spoke just one word, 'Come'. Peter stepped out onto the water and began to walk on it. Peter walked on the word of Christ, which enabled him to walk on the water.

When Christ speaks, his word is equal to the manifestation. We must hear the spoken word of Christ as well as spending time with the written word.

Returning to the story we can imagine what may have happened if the disciples had acted differently. 'Wait a minute. Don't worry. Jesus said that we would get to the other side.' The disciples questioned whether Jesus cared. Jesus does care.

> *Cast all your anxiety on him because he cares for you.* (1 Peter 5:7)

The promise is valuable to anyone who believes. The fulfilment will come. Just believe.

Jesus asked the disciples why they were so frightened. Why should they be? Jesus was with them. He would never leave or abandon them. Why was it that the disciples still had no faith? They had experienced Jesus' power. They had seen miracles. Jesus had not lost his power or stopped caring.

Today we must keep the faith. Obey the written and spoken word of Christ. Jesus is in our boat whether it is calm or stormy. He said:

> *'Surely I will be with you always, to the end of the age.'* (Matthew 28:20)

When Jesus calls us to go over to the other side he will go with us. He will deliver us across. He will see us through no matter what is thrown at us.

Remember, Jesus said 'Let us go over… together.'

Chapter 16

Perseverance

Happy is the Person who Does Not Lose Faith

One person with commitment, persistence and endurance will accomplish more than a thousand with interest alone. If you look at the life of anyone who has ever done anything significant they have had more than interest only. They had persistence.

Jesus said:

> *'Happy is the man who does not lose faith in me.'*

Keep and hold on to the faith

Civil rights leader Martin Luther King Jr (1928-1968), inspired and sustained the struggle for freedom, non-violence and social justice in America. He was totally committed to his cause. He endured hatred and extreme opposition. His persistent courage accomplished historical and significant changes. He, with others, brought greater equality and freedom to African-Americans. He persevered. Nothing could stop him. But on April 4th 1968, Dr King was assassinated by a sniper as he stood talking on the balcony of his second floor room at the Lorraine Hotel, Memphis. He died in hospital from a gun shot wound to the neck. His passion and principles inspired thousands to continue to work for equality and justice after his death. Even death could not stop the cause.

Nelson Mandela, the South African President, was instrumental in breaking down the apartheid system. In an attempt to stop his work, he was imprisoned for sixteen years. But he continued to inspire others from his prison cell. He persevered. Soon after his release from prison in 1990, government rule was given to the black majority and the system which had divided and destroyed lives was at last broken. The healing process has begun for South Africa. The long walk to freedom was worth it. British MP Sir David Steel said of Mandela's life:

> ... an unusual mixture of courage, persistence, tolerance and forgiveness.[1]

Fix Your Eyes

Christ was committed. He persisted. During his life and the three years of ministry, he endured hardship and hunger. He endured the cross. He endured people forsaking him. He was committed to the world.

If we are going to do anything significant, be successful and bear much fruit we need to develop the habit of being persistent.

Winston Churchill said:

> The nose of the bulldog is slanted backwards so he can continue to breathe without letting go. [2]

Whatever you do, do not let go. Do not lose faith. Fix your eyes on Jesus.

Now obviously we do not want to be persistent in something we should be letting go of. I have known people who are determined and very committed to endure someone or doing something that they should not even be going near. Lawrence Sterne made the distinction:

> Tis known as perseverance in a good cause and obstinacy in a bad one. [3]

There are occasions when we are involved in something that is good, however it may be that God wants us to do something else. We need wisdom.

Run With Perseverance

> *Therefore since we are surrounded by such a great
> cloud of witnesses let us throw off everything that hin-
> ders and the sin that so easily entangles, and let us run
> with perseverance the race marked out for us. Let us fix
> our eyes on Jesus, the author and perfecter of our faith.
> Who for the joy set before him endured the cross, scorn-
> ing it's shame and sat down at the right hand of the
> throne of God* (Hebrews 12:1-2).

Run with perseverance. Throw away all that hinders and
entangles.

In prayer we need to be asking, seeking and knocking. Jesus
urges:

> *'Ask and it will be given to you; seek and you will find;
> knock and the door will be opened to you. For everyone
> who asks receives; he who seeks finds; and to him who
> knocks, the door will be opened.'* (Matthew 7:7-8)

Keep asking, keep seeking, keep knocking.

I remember a remarkable student who was rewarded for her
persistence. She was a female student at Prospect College in
Ibadan, southern Nigeria. During an assembly where several
hundred students were present, Rev Samuel Folahan, Principal
of the College, awarded several grants to enable some of the
poorer students to have their fees paid. Once this was finished
everyone thought that that part of the assembly was over.
However this one female student got up out of her seat and
came to the front. All of the other students were seated. She
looked at the Principal. She quietly and politely asked for a
grant. The Principal stood firm and said 'No further grants
would be given that morning'. She continued to stand. She did
not move. He dismissed her and told her that she could not have
a grant. She would not go. She would not take 'No' for an
answer. Some of her student friends pleaded with him to give

her a grant. They continued to ask patiently. It lasted for several minutes. He finally gave in and rewarded her boldness with a grant. It is so important for us to be steadfast.

Persistence
by Calvin Coolidge

Nothing in the world can take the place of persistence.
Talent will not;
Nothing is more common than successful people with talent.
Genius will not;
Unrewarded genius is almost a proverb.
Education will not;
The world is full of educated derelicts.
Persistence and determination alone are omnipotent.
The slogan 'Press On'
Has solved and always will solve the problems of the human race. [4]

Asking, Seeking, Knocking

On one occasion, when I was preaching at Gospel meeting in Africa where several thousand gathered, hundreds came forward for prayer. As I began praying for one particular woman I felt that she needed deliverance from evil spirits. I told the evil spirits to go in the name of Jesus Christ. I knew that she was being set free. I persisted and kept on praying. I looked at her and asked God, What is happening here? Are they gone now? Is she free? I felt the Lord say to me 'No, carry on praying.' I continued in prayer on her behalf. She was quiet, seemingly at peace and free. I thought for a moment that the work was finished, but it was not, so I continued until she was completely liberated. During the testimony time she came to the platform and shared how she had been delivered and set free that evening. If I stopped praying too soon, it would not have happened. Persistence in prayer is the key.

Starting All Over Again

The famous scientist Sir Isaac Newton owned a dog called Diamond. Diamond did him a very bad turn. Newton had taken eight whole years to write a very important book. One morning he came into his room and found that Diamond had knocked over a candle and the candle had set fire to the book on his desk. Think what that meant; eight whole years of work burnt up, but he could not be angry with the dog that did not know what he was doing. Newton said, 'Diamond, little do you know the labour and trouble to which you have put your master.' He did not look upon that great work as lost for ever as most people would have done. He sat down at his desk to start all over again.

All of us face trials of some kind. Trials test the quality of our faith in God and in his word. Perseverance will develop within us as we trust during difficult times. As we allow this perseverance to finish its work we will become mature and complete, not lacking anything (James 1:2-4).

Run with perseverance, embracing God's calling and vision in your heart. Perseverance is available. Francis de Sales, author of *Introduction to the Devout Life*, rightly says:

> Though perseverance does not come from our power, yet it is within our power. [5]

Refuse to listen to the threats of your enemy. On his voyage which resulted in the discovery of America, Columbus refused to listen to the threats of his sailors. As day after day no land appeared, the sailors threatened to mutiny and demanded that they turn back. Columbus would not listen and each day entered two words in the Ship's log, 'sailed on'.

The Apostle Paul writing to the first century Christians urged them:

> ...*be on the alert with all perseverance* (Ephesians 6:18 NASB).

We can run the race of our lives because we know God watches over us.

The Race
by D. H. Groberg

1

'Quit! Give up! You're beaten!'
They shout at me and plead.
'There's just too much against you now.
This time you can't succeed!'

And as I start to hang my head
In front of failure's face,
My downward fall is broken by
The memory of a race.

And hope refills my weakened will
As I recall that scene;
For just the thought of that short race
Rejuvenates my being.

11

A children's race - young boys, young men
How I remember well.
Excitement, sure! But also fear;
It wasn't hard to tell.

They all lined up so full of hope;
Each thought to win that race.
Or tie for first, or if not that,
At least take second place.

And fathers watched from off the side,
Each cheering for his son.
And each boy hoped to show his dad
That he would be the one.

The whistle blew and off they went!
Young hearts and hopes afire.

To win and be the hero there
Was each young boy's desire.

And one boy in particular
Whose dad was in the crowd,
Was running near the lead and thought,
'My dad will be so proud!'

But as they speeded down the field
Across a shallow dip,
The little boy who thought to win
Lost his step and slipped.

Trying hard to catch himself
His hands flew out to brace,
And mid the laughter of the crowd
He fell flat on his face.

So down he fell and with him hope
He couldn't win it now –
Embarrassed, sad, he only wished
To disappear somehow.

But as he fell his dad stood up
And showed his anxious face
Which to the boy so clearly said:
'Get up and win the race.'

He quickly rose, no damage done.
Behind a bit, that's all –
And ran with all his mind and might
To make up for his fall.

So anxious to restore himself
To catch up and to win –
His mind went faster than his legs;
He slipped and fell again!

He wished then he had quit before
With only one disgrace.
'I'm hopeless as a runner now;
I shouldn't try to race.'

But in the laughing crowd he searched
And found his father's face.
That steady look which said again:
'Get up and win the race!'

So up he jumped to try again
Ten yards behind the last –
'If I'm to gain those yards,' he thought,
'I've got to move real fast.'

Exerting everything he had
He gained eight or ten
But trying so hard to catch the lead
He slipped and fell again!

Defeat! He lay there silently
A tear dropped from his eye –
'There's no sense running anymore;
Three strikes: I'm out! Why try?'

The will to rise had disappeared
All hope had fled away;
So far behind, so error prone;
A loser all the way.

'I've lost so what's the use,' he thought.
'I'll live with my disgrace.'
But then he thought about his dad
Who soon he'd have to face.

'Get up,' an echo sounded low.
'Get up and take your place;
You were not meant for failure here.

Get up and win the race.'

'With borrowed will, get up,' it said,
'You haven't lost at all,
For winning is no more than this:
To rise each time you fall.'

So up he rose to run once more,
And with a new commit
He resolved that win or lose
At least he wouldn't quit.

So far behind the others now,
The most he'd ever been –
Still he gave it all he had
And ran as though to win.

Three times he'd fallen, stumbling;
Three times he rose again;
Too far behind to hope to win
He still ran to the end.

They cheered the winning runner
As he crossed the line first place,
Head high, and proud, and happy;
No falling, no disgrace.

But when the fallen youngster
Crossed the line last place,
The crowd gave him the greater cheer
For finishing the race.

And even though he came in last
With head bowed low, unproud,
You would have thought he'd won the
Race to listen to the crowd.

And to his dad he sadly said,

'I didn't do so well.'
'To me, you won,' his father said.
'You rose each time you fell.'

111

And now when things seem dark and hard
And difficult to face,
The memory of that little boy
Helps me in my own race.

For all of life is like that race,
With ups and downs and all.
And all you have to do to win,
Is rise each time you fall.

'Quit! Give up! You're beaten!'
They still shout in my face.
But another voice within me says:
'Get up and win the race!' [6]

Chapter 17
Questions

Here are some excerpts from interviews I have given; the sort of questions I am often asked:

Q: What type of evangelism is effective in Britain today?

A: Evangelism that actually works is worth repeating. There are 101 different ways of presenting the good news of Jesus - one of the most effective methods I think for the local church is a meal-type event, such as restaurant evangelism. Our experience has been that people will come to such events; in fact, all events with food work well! Guests coming to such a 'meeting' don't feel threatened or embarrassed, the neutral venue makes it easier for them.

For too long the church has asked people to come to church. Why? Jesus said to go out! Jesus often met with friends and colleagues, in their homes, for meals, where he would be the guest speaker. We must be willing to do anything to get the good news of Jesus across, regardless of the cost.

Traditional door-to-door work can work well, especially for Anglican churches. I have found it effective because a lot of people, if they had to say what religion they were, would say Church of England. I would knock on the door and say something like:

> Hello, my name is Andy, this is Sarah, and we are from Christ Church. You're in our parish, so we have come here to ask you if we can be of any help?

Simple isn't it?

I visited one road for six years and it took that long to know the people. It was my responsibility, I prayed along it, knocked on the doors and got to know the people. If you and I went door-to-door in that road today, you would find that the majority of those people still remember me, they would say:

> We haven't seen you for a long time, you used to come regularly.

Actually, we tend give up too easily - we ought to keep going. The Alpha course also works well, but usually one thing is not enough. It's not a question of Alpha or restaurant outreaches or friendship or big celebration meetings or guest meetings. We should try many different ways as people respond to different things.

Q: What evangelism in Europe has impressed you?

A: I once saw a wonderful example travelling on a train in Greece, from Piraeus to Athens. I was with a pastor of a church called the Lighthouse and he said, 'On the way on the train I'll evangelise.' He stood up in the train and spoke: 'Forgive me that I don't know much Greek, but I want to speak about Christ.'

He spoke for about five to ten minutes while I watched all the people out the corner of my eye to see how they were responding They sat there very politely with their arms folded, just minding their own business, as if he wasn't doing anything - but I could see they were listening. There was no heckling, no shouting. He finished, thanked everybody for listening and then he started giving out leaflets - and spontaneous conversations started breaking out.

Now, that that kind of evangelism works well in Greece, because it's almost part of the culture - after he had finished speaking, a lady got up and started begging for money, and she had an official pass to do it! That was also perfectly acceptable.

Q: Where have you found open-air evangelism successful?

A: In Greece. There is a very different response to open air evangelism there, and it works. I have taken teams from England to work with evangelical churches there. We would drive to a town in northern Greece, for example Eddessa; we would set up the PA, get permission from a restaurant to plug the amplifier in, throw the wire across the stream and then we would begin.

Impressionist Dave Edwards went down very well, impersonating Elvis Presley, Mick Jagger and Michael Jackson. People are curious, intrigued, interested. Then mime artists John and Carina Persson, who are outstanding, would perform. They captivate and entertain. Every mime sketch has a particular message.

Then I went on with an interpreter to preach for 15 minutes. By this time, there may be 300 people gathered around, including a lot of young people and they listen to the Gospel. This has happened in a variety of different towns and villages in the North of Greece with a very fruitful response.

Q: Do you evangelise spontaneously?

A: Yes, I believe there is power in the Gospel, so I will share it as often as possible with people. They deserve to hear. People need to have an opportunity to hear and know about Jesus Christ who loves them and can make a really worthwhile difference in their lives.

In my early Christian years, sharing Jesus spontaneously was the only kind of evangelism I knew and did.

One day, when I was a student studying engineering, I was waiting at a bus stop after a day at college and I noticed a middle-aged man dressed very poorly, looking in a waste bin. There and then I bought some food for him and presented it to him. He agreed to meet me a few days later, when we had a meal together and talked. John had been in an accident and now suffered from multiple sclerosis. Over the next seven months we became friends and he would often show me photographs of himself as a young man while on holiday, travelling around on his motorbike. Eventually John became a Christian and I took him to church. I was really glad to have the chance to know him and introduce him to Christ.

I have shared Jesus with people on the train, to the waiters in restaurants, and when people come to my home, like my insurance man. One young sales woman came to our door once and, after we spoke for a while, I presented her with a book explaining how she could find peace and happiness with God. She gladly took it, asking me questions about being a Christian.

Q: You go to Nigeria often; how are church services there?

A: Meetings in Nigeria are charged with expectancy and highly focussed on the needs of the congregations. The people don't hesitate to respond to a message - they believe God will help them, and they want their leaders to pray for them. The people love it; you can see it on their faces. I haven't seen responses quite like this anywhere else.

When I am preaching, whether to small groups or to many thousands, there is faith. I remind them that Christ is the same today as yesterday and they stream forward for prayer - people are healed and delivered.

Since my first visit in 1991 I have mostly been involved with the Christ Apostolic Churches in Ibadan and Lagos, one of Nigeria's largest churches. Led by Dr Rev S. K. Abiara and Rev Samuel Folahan, the church oversees dozens of small satellite churches throughout the country, plus others in Athens, New York, Ontario and London. The churches in Ibadan and Lagos number many thousands. At the Christmas Jesus Festival - a two week event - up to 30,000 people attend. There are special healing and revival meetings. Leaders and the people are expectant that the Lord will heal and save, and the Lord does heal and save.

Q: Are African attitudes different from those in Britain?

A: Yes. One is the whole issue of giving. There is great hardship, high unemployment and an enormous struggle to find enough to eat - yet individuals in the churches are generous, believing that giving money for God's work is as important as worshipping Him. People dance their way to the front of the church meeting and drop their money in buckets, often with three or four collections in one meeting. It is a happy and hilarious occasion.

This is one of the reasons, I believe, why they are experiencing revival, growth and healing in their Church. They give. In his book *The Gift of Giving*, Dr R.T. Kendall quotes O.S. Hawkins as saying:

> The principal hindrance to the advancement of the Kingdom of God is greed. It is the chief obstacle to heaven-sent revival. It seems that when the back of greed is broken, the human spirit soars into regions of unselfishness. I believe it is safe to say there can be no continuous revival without 'hilarious' giving. And I fear no contradiction - wherever there is 'hilarious' giving there will soon be revival.

It is true; the sooner we Christians learn the joy of giving out of what we have - the sooner we will experience God's blessing in every area of our lives and churches.

Q: Is there anything we can learn from Nigerian church leadership?

A: Nigerian Christians really honour one another; I have never seen it quite the same anywhere else - and it is clearly revealed in their services. Established church leaders give the up-and-coming young leaders space and opportunity to develop - with an average life expectancy of just 51 years for men and 54 for women they take future leaders more seriously then we do in Britain.

In any one meeting there may be ten or twelve individuals involved at the front. There are at least two preachers and two or three service leaders. You see, they strongly believe in spiritually 'fathering' children - the main leaders are nurturing younger leaders all the time. We should learn from this.

Also evangelists in the churches are regarded with enormous esteem, with Christ Apostolic Church running two Bible colleges, one exclusively training evangelists!

Q: Are the mass conversions we hear about in Africa genuine?

A: Everything I have been involved in leads me to believe so.

I have heard Christians criticise the follow-up to conversions in Africa as being weak, and they lay blame to some of the tremendous work done by the likes of Reinhard Bonnke and others, saying many are converted but few come through. That has never been my experience. I have been with Reinhard in Ethiopia and have seen first hand the extent to which Nigerian churches disciple and nurture their new believers.

Those that come forward to receive Christ in meetings are all taken to one side where church stewards take their details. The new converts are baptised just a few days later, as in New Testament times, then encouraged to attend church and are taught very well in their adult Sunday school. There is always a genuine response when the real gospel of Jesus crucified is preached.

Chapter 18

Relationships

Relationships can make a huge difference to the quality of our lives. Some people are better at relationships than others. If you want to have a friend you need to be a friend.

Mentoring

A mentor is an experienced and trusted advisor. Paul Stanley and J. Robert Clinton define mentoring as follows:

> Mentoring is a relational experience in which one person empowers another by sharing God-given resources. [1]

A mentor empowers another person. At present I am mentoring three younger evangelists. This is done through encouragement, visits, fellowship (sometimes over a meal), taking an interest, caring and prayer. Mentoring these evangelists is sharing my God-given resources. An underlying attitude towards them is that I strongly believe in them. I believe in their ability and their potential. All three occasionally telephone requesting help of some kind, and because I am committed to them I always try to help.

Mentoring others takes up time and energy. As a result of these mentoring relationships, three evangelists have had their ministries strengthened and they have been built up.

For example, Joseph accompanied me on a preaching visit to Nigeria. He witnessed dynamic, vibrant ministry on a large scale. He saw poverty, disease and sickness. He returned to England having learnt important lessons.

Steve has published his first book and will soon have another, both inspired because of the mentoring relationship.

Mentoring can happen anywhere, as Bobb Biehl and Glen Urquhart point out:

Most mentoring takes place in a very relaxed setting as it did centuries ago in fatherly apprenticeships ... walking, sailing, golfing, driving ... anywhere you are with your mentor or your protégé.

Mentoring often happens ten minutes at a time... here and there as you move through life together. Don't see mentoring as all work. It often involves the joy of mutual sharing. Mentoring happens more in the context of a relationship than a formal class room. Mentoring is a life attitude as much as a formal structure. It can be even more enjoyable as you are doing things you enjoy together! [2]

According to these authors, mentoring is:

Making the mentor's personal strength, resources, and network (friendship/contacts) available to help a protégé reach his or her goals.[3]

A mentor is someone who is helping another to reach a goal. Anyone can be a mentor. Anyone can be mentored. Mentoring can be seen in the Bible.

Dr Ted W. Engstrom in his book *The Fine Art of Mentoring* says this about the mentoring style of Jesus:

Unlike mentors who are considered successful today, Jesus did not organise his team in order to be served. He never asked them to make him look good. They were never required to wait on him. Just the opposite was true: he served them. The Master built them up, encouraged them, corrected them and stretched them as they struggled to receive the truth and obey the will of God. 'Whoever wants to become great among you must be your servant,' he taught in Mark 10:43-45, '*and whoever wants to be first must be the slave of all. For even the Son of Man did not come to be served, but to serve, and to give his life as a ransom for many.*' In John 13:15, he said in the upper room after washing their feet, '*I have set you an example that you should do as I have done for you.*' [4]

The Apostle Paul Mentored Timothy

Paul was a spiritual father to Timothy. Paul wrote to Timothy:

To Timothy, my true son in the faith... (1 Timothy 1:2),

And again he affectionately wrote:

To Timothy, my dear son... (2 Timothy 1:2)

Paul had a fatherly mentoring relationship toward Timothy. Timothy became strong and reached his goal because of Paul's input. He received great encouragement from Paul's two wonderful letters.

We need mentors like Paul. Timothy was a pastor of a church with a secondary calling and gift of doing the work of an evangelist. Paul constantly spurred this younger leader on to greater things, 'You can do it, go for it, God believes in you, I believe in you.'

Timothy was timid and fearful in temperament. This did not disqualify him from leadership within the Church. Neither did it affect his ministry. However Paul was always lifting him up with wise words and advice. Paul was constantly urging him to press through the fears he had.

Timothy was a humble, likeable and respectable pastor. He had great potential and Paul knew that. Paul saw the calling of God upon Timothy's life. Paul reminds Timothy of the prophecies the Church had given to him. Paul told him to follow the words given and use them. Paul told Timothy to hold on to the faith and to continue with his good conscience (1 Timothy 1:18-19). Paul gave Timothy instructions (1Timothy 2:1-15). Timothy is encouraged to command and teach certain things in the Church.

Paul tells Timothy not to let anyone look down on him because he is young. Paul encouraged him to be an example to the believers both in his speech, life, love, faith, and purity. Paul instructed Timothy to devote himself to the public reading of scripture, preaching, and teaching (1 Timothy 4:11-14). He told

Timothy not to neglect his gift. Paul called him 'a man of God'.

Paul charged Timothy, his beloved son in the Lord, to preach the Gospel and care for the Church (1 Timothy 6:11,14). Timothy was encouraged to guard everything that has been entrusted to him (2 Timothy 6:20).

In Paul's second letter he continues to mentor young Timothy:

> *For this reason I remind you to fan into flame the gift*
> *of God, which is in you through the laying on of hands.*
> *For God did not give us a spirit of timidity, but a spirit*
> *of power, of love and of self-discipline.*
> (2 Timothy 1:6-7)

Writing to the Corinthian Christians Paul tells them how he feels about Timothy:

> *For this reason I am sending you Timothy, my son*
> *whom I love, who is faithful in the Lord. He will*
> *remind you of my way of life in Christ Jesus which*
> *agrees with what I teach everywhere in every church.*
> (1 Corinthians 4:17)

To the Christians at Philippi, Paul makes his relationship with Timothy clear:

> *I have no one else like him, who takes a genuine inter-*
> *est in your welfare.* (Philippians 2:20)

Paul longed to see Timothy, (2 Timothy 1:14), and asked him twice to come (2 Timothy 4:9, 21).

Timothy would always be Paul's son in the Lord and the mentoring process would continue from the great apostle to the younger pastor. As Timothy matured he was able to have an input in Paul's life. The two church leaders had a true respect for one another. The mentoring process was now two-way because Timothy was able to encourage Paul.

We need several people to mentor us. Each one giving us something different.

Intensive mentoring requires frequent time together.

In an occasional mentoring situation the time given is less. A few meetings together may be all that is required. There may be the need to meet only once a year. It may require time together as and when needed. There is great flexibility and space for creativity - there are no rigid, set rules.

There have been occasions when I have had up to four mentors, of the occasional type. One occasional mentor I would see two or three times a year.

In their book *Connecting: The Mentoring Relationships You Need to Succeed in Life*, authors Paul D. Stanley and J. Robert Clinton, define and show different types of mentoring.

Within intensive mentoring there are three kinds:

- The Discipler
- The Spiritual Guide
- The Coach

Stanley and Clinton define the Discipler:

> Discipling is a relational process in which a more experienced follower of Christ shares with a new believer the commitment, understanding, and basic skills necessary to know and obey Jesus Christ as Lord. [5]

They define the Spiritual Guide and the Coach as:

> A Spiritual Guide is a godly, mature follower of Christ who shares knowledge, skills, and basic philosophy on what it means to increasingly realise Christlikeness in all areas of life. [6]
>
> The Coach's central thrust is to provide motivation and impart skills and application to meet a task or challenge. [7]

Intensive mentoring could mean that one person is the Discipler, Spiritual Guide and Coach. It could be that two or three people provide what is needed by the individual. The mentoree could have one Discipler, one Spiritual Guide, and one Coach.

Occasional mentoring is done by:

- The Counsellor
- The Teacher
- The Sponsor.

Stanley and Clinton define each of these as follows:

> The central thrust of a Counsellor is timely advice and impartial perspective on the mentoree's view of self, others, circumstances, and ministry. [8]
>
> The central thrust of a teacher-mentor is to impart knowledge and understanding of a particular subject. [9]
>
> Sponsorship is a relational process in which a mentor having credibility and positional or spiritual authority within an organisation or network relates to a mentoree not having those resources so as to enable development of the mentoree and the mentoree's influence in the organisation. [10]

One person maybe able to mentor, offering all three aspects outlined above. It more likely that two or more people will be needed to fulfil the needs of the individual.

There are those within the Church that can only offer mentoring skills as a counsellor. Others are able to mentor acting as a Counsellor and Teacher.

Mentoring someone maybe for a season. The season can vary in time. The Church desperately needs mentors. We need to see the value in empowering and resourcing others. Mentoring means that you are committed to seeing the other person grow and reach their potential.

> You can become a mentor ... helping someone succeed who has high leadership potential, but less experience than you have. [11] (Biehl and Urquhart)

Mentoring is not using another person to accomplish your goals. Be warned.

> 'Mentoring is not helping you become another me! Rather it is helping you become a fully developed you.' [12]. (Biehl and Urquhart)

Mentoring can take place at a distance by telephone, fax, letter, computer, and occasional visits.

For mentoring to work properly there must be accountability. This will help to enable the individual to reach their full potential. The degree of accountability will vary with each situation.

There is another kind of mentoring which is accomplished in small groups. This can have an advantage over individual mentoring. I have been involved in mentoring men and women through the use of small groups. This was helpful because I was able to train women without the obvious dangers that can sometimes occur.

Mentoring can happen at almost any age:

- Young adults in their late teens can mentor younger teenagers.

- Woman are encouraged to mentor younger women in Titus 2:4-5:
  Then they can train the younger women to love their husbands and children, to be self-controlled and pure, to be busy at home, to be kind, and to be subject to their husbands, so that no one will malign the word of God.

- Men are encouraged to help and train younger men in 2 Timothy 2:2.

Usually it is safe for men to mentor men and woman to mentor women. However relationships can go wrong between those of the same sex as with those of the opposite sex.

Don't Cross the Line in Relationships

A married pastor decided to help a woman in his church who
needed counselling. He arranged to meet her alone. That was a
serious mistake. He had now got onto the roof as David had in
the Old Testament story. They were attracted to one another
and later became emotionally involved. To guard against this
danger they should have met with another person present,
preferably the pastor's wife. One wrong move led to another
and eventually the pastor left his wife for the other woman. He
is no longer pastoring the church.

Two men shared a house together. An occasion arose where one
gave the other a massage. After a period of weeks inappropriate
behaviour began between the two of them. The consequences for
those close to them and for themselves was disastrous.

Mary Pytches in her book, *Between Friends*, speaks about limitations in friendships:

> Even when, apparently, there seems to be no need to
> implement precautions in a pastoral situation, it is wise to
> remind oneself occasionally of the limitations which must
> naturally belong to a married person.
>
> At separate conferences two women told me almost
> identical stories. Both were married to lay-men with some
> pastoral oversight in their local church. Recently, howev-
> er, each man had become very friendly with another man
> in the church. In one case the relationship had begun
> through one man seeking advise from the other. Since
> then most evenings of the week the new friend had was
> either ensconced in the husband's study or they spent the
> evening together in the other man's flat. They would talk
> together until late into the night and even occasionally
> into the early hours of the morning, while the wife sat
> alone. She knew, as did the other wife, that her company
> was not welcome and that she was excluded from the
> relationship. A deep intimate friendship had grown up
> through a normal pastoral concern.

The two ladies who spoke to me knew that their husbands were investing more emotional energy with their new friends than with them. These men had done nothing obviously wrong morally and yet anyone viewing the relationships would have queried the rightness of the situation. [13]

We must be aware that there are limitations between what we should and should not do. Many believe that could 'never happen to me'. History shows that there have been some great men and women who have fallen. Although forgiveness is granted the effects of our sin can be devastating. We must keep a constant eye on our hearts and motives. There are limitations on all of us. We must have boundaries in place that we do not cross. Mary Pytches writes:

This opens up an important question. How much is a close friendship available to a married person outside of the marriage? Obviously between members of the opposite sex the situational and emotional boundaries should be set at a safe distance. However, between members of the same sex a friendship can be very enriching. Yet as we have seen, friendship, even between married people of the same sex, can be fraught with dangers. Boundaries, as always, are the key. Two important boundaries should be implemented. One limiting the amount of time spent in each other's company, and the other limiting the amount of affection shown to one another. For one partner to spend many hours exclusively in the company of another person has to be detrimental to a marriage. Also, though some people are very extrovert in their show of affection, I would suggest that frequent touching and hugging in private would be inappropriate, however harmless it may seem. Many people, especially women I have counselled, have become homosexually involved unintentionally. The friendship went wrong, as I have already illustrated, when quite innocently at first, they began to express their affection for one another and in private. [14]

Qualities of a Mentor and Mentoree

What qualities should you look for in a mentor? When a mentor is considering mentoring someone they need to identify certain qualities in that person. Here is a helpful check list of what to look for in a mentor and in a mentoree:

Mentor Checklist: Before you choose a mentor, check to see they have these qualities:

- Will the mentor be objective, lovingly honest, and a balanced source of feed-back for your questions?

- Will the mentor be open and transparent with their own struggles?

- Will the mentor model their teachings?

- Does the mentor know you and believe in you?

- Will the mentor teach you as well as answer your questions?

- Is the mentor faithful in your eyes?

- Will the mentor be open to two-way communication … learning from you on occasions as well as teaching you?

- Does the mentor want to see younger people succeed in developing their spiritual and leadership potential?

Mentoree Checklist: Before you choose a mentoree, check to see if they have these qualities:

- Will you be able to believe in the mentoree?

- Do you naturally enjoy communicating with the mentoree?

- Will you be able to give without reservation to the mentoree?

- Will you love them as a brother or sister?

- Do you admire their potential as a leader?

- Is the mentoree teachable and eager to learn from you and mature in their spiritual and leadership potential?

- Does the mentoree admire you, as a mentor?

- Is the mentoree self-motivated even though not always confident?

- Will the mentoree be threatened by you or threatening to you?

Covenant Relationships

David had just killed Goliath the giant. He came before King Saul holding Goliath's head. Saul's son Jonathan listened as David and the King spoke together. The Bible says that once they had finished speaking Jonathan became one in spirit with David (1 Samuel 18:2).

> *And Jonathan made a covenant with David because he loved him as himself* (1 Samuel 18:3).

This covenant was initiated by Jonathan. The terms of the agreement are not detailed. It is certain that a promise of loyalty and friendship was given and agreed upon. Jonathan seals the agreement by symbolically giving David his robe, tunic, sword, bow and belt.

A covenant is a contract either verbal or in writing with a seal of agreement. A covenant relationship is an agreement with a commitment.

The bride and groom make a covenant with each other

through their wedding vows. It is an agreement and commitment to each other to love, honour and cherish, for better, for worse, for richer, for poorer, in sickness and in health, till death do us part. Rings are exchanged to symbolise the giving and receiving of the covenant between them.

When David had killed Goliath there had been singing and dancing:

> *'Saul has slain his thousands, and David his tens of thousands.'* (1 Samuel 18:7)

David was fast becoming popular, more so than Saul. The King saw what was happening and became jealous of David. Saul kept his eye on David (1 Samuel 18:9). An evil spirit came upon Saul and twice he tried to kill David with a spear (1 Samuel 18:10-11).

Saul was also afraid of David because he could see that the Lord was with him. Saul knew that the Lord had left him. Again Saul tried to kill David (1 Samuel 19). Later he unsuccessfully pursued him (1 Samuel 23).

David asked Jonathan:

> *'What have I done? What is my crime? How have I wronged your father, that he is trying to take my life?'* (1 Samuel 20:1)

Jonathan was not going to let an innocent man die and he reassured David that he will not let Saul kill him. Protection is promised to David:

> *So Jonathan made a covenant with the house of David, saying, 'May the Lord call David's enemies to account.' And Jonathan had David reaffirm his oath out of love for him as he loved him as himself* (1 Samuel 20 :16-17).

When Saul found out that Jonathan was protecting David he was furious.

> *Saul's anger flared up at Jonathan and he said to him, 'You*
> *son of a perverse and rebellious woman! Don't I know that*
> *you have sided with the son of Jesse to your own shame and*
> *to the shame of the mother who bore you? As long as the son*
> *of Jesse lives on this earth, neither you or your kingdom will*
> *be established. Now send and bring him to me, for he must*
> *die!' 'Why should he be put to death? What has he done?*
> *Jonathan asked his father.'* (1 Samuel 30:30-32)

Saul was not having any of this and hurled his spear at
Jonathan to kill him. Jonathan escaped and knew beyond a
doubt that Saul intended to kill David.

When David and Jonathan met the next morning they wept
together. Jonathan renewed his commitment to David, saying:

> *'Go in peace, for we have sworn friendship with each*
> *other in the name of the Lord, saying, "the Lord is wit-*
> *ness between you and me, and between your descendants*
> *and my descendants forever".' Then David left and*
> *Jonathan went back to the town* (1 Samuel 20:42).

Covenant friendships are not the ordinary kind of friendships
we have with many people. Covenant friendships must not be
entered into without careful consideration. Often a friendship
of this kind happens between two people gradually. The degree
of covenant friendship that existed between Jonathan and
David was of the highest kind and was rather unusual.

To have friends, you have to be friendly. It is far better to give
than to receive. You will find that if you love somebody for their
own sake, you will receive in return, perhaps in ways you have
never dreamed of.

Chapter 19

Samaritans Story

The story of the good Samaritan told by Jesus nearly 2000 years ago, is one of the most well known throughout the world today (Luke 10:25-37). Even those of other faiths and cultures know the story.

Although I have known the story and its meaning since I was a young boy, it did not take on significance until I was much older. As a young man I heard Christ knocking on the door of my heart and I decided to surrender my life to him. There was a definite and specific turn around, literally overnight, a turning to Christ's teachings and his ways.

For over twenty years I have practised the parable of the good Samaritan in different ways with many people. However it has been during the last few years that the force of Jesus' teaching to love our neighbour as ourselves has hit me the hardest. I have come to see that the core of Christianity is to love our neighbour as ourselves and to love God. By not loving our neighbour we neglect the very essence of Christianity. The essence of the life of Christ on earth was to love and serve broken humanity.

He Passed Over To The Other Side

A scholar well versed in scripture, an expert in the law, asked a question to test Jesus. He wanted to either take issue with Jesus or simply to see what kind of teacher he was.

'Teacher, what must I do to inherit eternal life?'

In response Jesus said:

'What is written in the law and how do you read it?'

The expert answered:

'Love the Lord you God with all your heart and with all your soul and with all your strength and with all your mind, and, love your neighbour as yourself.' (Luke 10:27)

The man answered correctly and was encouraged by Jesus to do exactly that. By doing so he would receive eternal life. The expert was not satisfied. He wanted to justify himself and therefore asked Jesus to explain who his neighbour was. Jesus then told a parable. Jesus frequently taught by telling a story or a parable. Here he paints a beautiful picture to show 'Who is my neighbour?'

A certain man was going down from Jerusalem to Jericho which was a distance of 17 miles and a descent from 25,000 feet above sea level to about 800 feet below sea level. The road ran through rocky, desert country, which provided places for robbers to attack defenceless travellers.

He did indeed fall into the hands of robbers. They stripped him of his clothes, beat him and went away, leaving him half dead.

A priest happened to be going down the same road and when he saw the man he passed by the other side. The priest was a Jewish man of the same religion and background as the wounded man lying on the road, in other words one of his own. It made no difference. You would think it would have, but it did not. He was a priest, he should have had compassion. In the story Jesus makes it very clear that, for the priest, there was no option but to stop and help. Instead he passed on the other side even though he saw a man bleeding to death.

A Levite, that is a lay associate, came to the place and saw the man, and he also passed on the other side.

This unfortunate individual experienced physical abuse from the hands of robbers. He had become a victim of thieves The robbers took easy advantage of a defenceless person minding his business. If that was not bad enough, he also suffered neglect from those who should have known better. The priest and Levite were after all supposed to be dedicated to serving God and people. He was a victim of the priest and Levite, his countrymen.

Love Somebody

A Samaritan came to where the man was. When he saw him he took pity on him. He went to him and bandaged his wounds, pouring in oil and wine. These had healing properties that would bring relief from pain and heal the wounds. Then he put the man on his own donkey. He was willing to be inconvenienced. He took him to an inn and continued to take care of him, staying the night. The next day the good Samaritan took out two silver coins, which was two day's pay, and gave them to the innkeeper. He instructed the innkeeper to look after him and that he would return and pay the balance for any extra expense.

Two silver coins, in those days, would have enabled a person to stay up to three months at an inn. The Samaritan was exceedingly lavish in the love he showed towards the wounded man. It was love that knew no bounds. The good Samaritan was willing to change his programme. He was flexible. More importantly his heart was full of compassion toward another. We read:

> But a Samaritan, as he travelled, came to a place where he was; when he saw him, he took pity on him. He went to him and bandaged his wounds ... (Luke 10:33-34)

Jesus finishes the story by asking the expert in the law:

> 'Which of the three do you think was a neighbour to the man who fell into the hands of the robbers?'
> The expert in the law replied, 'The man who had mercy on him.'
> Jesus told him, 'Go and do likewise.' (Luke 10:36-37)

It is significant that the person Jesus commended was neither the religious leader - the priest or the Levite, but a hated foreigner. Jews viewed Samaritans as half-breeds, both physically and spiritually. Samaritans and Jews practiced open hostility, but Jesus asserted that love knows no nationality boundaries.

Nothing should get in the way of us loving our neighbour as ourselves. It is the core of Christianity to love our neighbour.

This kind of love is practical. It is love in action. It comes from an unselfish person who is moved by pity when they see suffering. Dr Martin Luther King Jr., the civil rights leader and Baptist minister, gave his life for those who were victimised by others. King certainly loved his neighbour as himself. He loved people whatever their background, colour or culture. Throughout his life, Martin Luther King Jr showed wonderful qualities as did the Samaritan in the story Christ told.

On February 4th 1968 at the age of 39, two months before Martin Luther King Jr was assassinated, he preached a prophetic and highly personal sermon from the pulpit of Ebenezer Baptist Church. At the end of the sermon he encourages his listeners to love their neighbour, to be committed to those who suffer from injustice, sheer neglect or prejudice. This is what he said:

> Every now and then I guess we all think realistically about that day when we will be victimised with what is life's final common denominator- that something we call death. We all think about it. And every now and then I think about my own death and I think about my own funeral. And I don't think of it in a morbid sense. Every now and then I ask myself. 'What is it that I would want said?' And I leave the word with you this morning.
>
> If any of you are around when I have to meet my day, I don't want a long funeral. And if you get somebody to deliver the eulogy, tell them not to talk too long. Every now and then I wonder what I want them to say. Tell them not to mention I have a Nobel Peace Prize. That isn't important. Tell them not to mention that I have three or four hundred other awards, that's not important. Tell him not to mention where I went to school.
>
> I'd like somebody to mention that day, that Martin Luther King Jr, tried to give his life serving others. I'd like for somebody to say that day, that Martin Luther King Jr, tried to love somebody. I want you to say that day, that I tried to be right on the war question. I want you to be able to say that day, that I did try to feed the hungry. And

I want you to be able to say that day, that I did try, in my life, to clothe those who were naked. I want you to say, on that day, that I did try, in my life, to visit those who were in prison. I want you to say that I tried to love and serve humanity.

Yes, if you want to say that I was a drum major, say that I was a drum major for justice; say that I was a drum major for peace; I was a drum major for righteousness. And all of the other shallow things will not matter. I won't have any money to leave behind. I won't have the fine and luxurious things of life to leave behind. But I just want to leave a committed life behind.

And that's all I want to say... If I can help somebody as I pass along, if I can cheer somebody with a word or song, if I can show somebody he's travelling wrong, then my living will not be in vain. If I can do my duty as a Christian ought, if I can bring salvation to a world once wrought, if I can spread the message as the master taught, then my living will not be in vain'. [1]

What an inspiration this is to us to keep on serving God and others.

Chapter 20

Thinking Matters

What Do You Think?

Naaman was the Commander of the Syrian army (2 Kings 5:1-15). He was highly respected by the king of Syria. He was a great soldier. However, he suffered from leprosy, a dreaded skin disease. Naaman's wife had a young Israelite servant girl. One day the servant told her mistress that she knew of a prophet in Samaria who could cure Naaman. Naaman heard of this and spoke to the king about it. The king of Syria sent Naaman to the king of Israel, with a letter of introduction asking him to heal Naaman. He also sent a large amount of money. When the king of Israel read the letter he tore his clothes in despair because he knew he did not have the power to heal. He thought that the king of Syria wanted to start a quarrel.

Elisha the prophet heard of the difficulty. He intervened and asked that Naaman be sent to him. Elisha wanted to use this opportunity to show Naaman that there was a prophet of God in Israel. Naaman went with his chariots and horses and stopped at the entrance to Elisha's house. Elisha sent one of his servants out to Naaman to tell him to go and wash seven times in the River Jordan. This would cure him of the disease. Naaman went away angry and said:

> 'I thought that he would surely come out to me and stand and call on the name of the Lord his God, wave his hand over the spot and cure me of leprosy.'

Naaman turned away and went away in a rage.

Naaman had some excellent friends who respectfully reasoned with him. He listened to their wise counsel and decided to go to the River Jordan and wash himself as the prophet had said. His skin became healthy, like that of a child. Naaman was very thankful to Elisha and returned to him with his men and said:

> 'Now I know that there is no God in all the world except in Israel.'

All's well that ends well. It was nearly not to be when Naaman said, 'I thought that he would surely come out to me...' Naaman thought but he thought wrong. Naaman then changed his mind.

Sometimes we think the way we think does not matter, but it does. In the book of Proverbs we read:

> For as he thinks within himself, so he is. (Proverbs 23:7 NASB)

It was the prophet Isaiah, who came after Elisha, who wrote these words about God's thoughts and God's ways:

> 'For my thoughts are not your thoughts,
> neither are your ways my ways,'
> declares the Lord.
> 'As the heavens are higher than the earth,
> so are my ways higher than your ways
> and my thoughts than your thoughts.'
> (Isaiah 55:8-9)

In Naaman's case he thought that Elisha should come out to see him not send a servant. He thought that Elisha should pray and wave his hand over him, so that he would be healed. Naaman thought that the Rivers of Abana and Pharpar in Damascus were better than the River Jordan in Israel. Surely it would be better for him to wash in them, he thought. Our thinking matters. What would have happened if Naaman had not changed his mind? He would have remained a leper.

Think Big

If you think you are beaten, you are,
If you think you dare not, you daren't.
If you'd like to win, but you think you can't
It's almost a cinch you won't.
If you think you'll lose, you're lost
For out in the world you'll find
Success begins with a fellow's will -
It's all in the state of the mind.

For many a race is lost
Before ever a step is run,
And many a coward fails
Before ever his work's begun.
Think big and your deeds will grow,
Think small and you'll fall behind,
Think that you can and you will,
It's all in the state of the mind.

If you think you're outclassed, you are,
You've got to think high to rise.
You've got to be sure of yourself
Before you can win the prize.
Life's battles don't always go
To the stronger or faster man,
But soon or late the man who wins
Is the fellow who thinks he can.

They Thought, But Thought Wrong

Samuel was seeking to anoint God's chosen one (1 Samuel 16:1-13). God instructed him to go to Bethlehem and invite Jesse to a sacrifice. God would then show him which of Jesse's sons he was to anoint as king of Israel. When Samuel saw the sons of Jesse, Eliab stood out from them. Samuel thought, *'Surely the Lord's anointed stands here before me.'*

> *But the Lord said to Samuel, 'Do not consider his appear-*
> *ance or his height, for I have rejected him. The Lord does*
> *not look at the things man looks at. Man looks at the out-*
> *ward appearance, but the Lord looks at the heart.'* (1
> Samuel 16:7)

Jesse calls for another of his sons. Abinadab passed in front of Samuel. Samuel knew that God had not chosen him. Shammah passed in front of Samuel. He was not the chosen one. Seven sons of Jesse passed in front of Samuel, but none of them were the Lord's chosen. Samuel asked Jesse if he had any more sons? There was David who was looking after the sheep. He was the youngest and a shepherd boy. Surely it could not be him, could it? David was sent for. The Lord told Samuel that David was his chosen one. Samuel anointed David with oil and from that day on the Spirit of the Lord was on him with power.

When Samuel saw Eliab, he thought, 'Surely the Lord's anointed stands here before me.' Samuel thought, but thought wrong. It was a good thing that Samuel was open to hear God. Samuel heard God and changed his mind. If you change your mind, you change your life and the lives of others.

God spoke to Moses and told him how he felt about his people Israel, who were suffering under the harsh Egyptian slave drivers. God told Moses to go to Pharaoh and bring the Israelites out of Egypt. Moses said to God:

> *'Who am I, that I should go to Pharaoh and bring the*
> *Israelites out of Egypt?'* (Exodus 3:11)

Later, Moses said to God:

> *'O Lord, I have never been eloquent, neither in the past*
> *nor since you have spoken to your servant. I am slow of*
> *speech and tongue.'* (Exodus 4:10)

These were the thoughts of Moses. He thought wrong. In the end Moses changed his mind. He obeyed God. Moses became the liberator for a whole nation. Israel finally got into the promised land. Changing your mind changes your life.

The Apostle Peter one day was praying on the roof (Acts 10:9-23). He fell into a deep sleep and has a vision. He saw heaven opened and a large sheet coming to earth. The sheet contains all kinds of four footed animals, reptiles of the earth and birds. He hears a voice telling him to get up, to kill and eat.

> *'Surely not, Lord!' Peter replied 'I have never eaten any-thing impure or unclean'*
> *The voice spoke to Peter a second time, 'Do not call any-thing impure that God had made clean.'*
> *This happened three times and immediately the sheet was taken back to heaven* (Acts 10:14-16).

Peter woke up and thought about the meaning of this vision. God was showing Peter that he wanted to give the good news of Jesus and the Holy Spirit to all people (Acts 11:17-18). Until this time the Gospel and the Holy Spirit had only been received by Jewish people. God had shown Peter that he was about to pour his Spirit on the Gentiles. Peter was to baptise these new Christians, who were to receive God's grace. These people were also to be part of the Church. God showed Peter that he does not show favouritism. All people can benefit from the good news of Jesus. All people can receive new life by the Spirit (Acts 10,11).

Peter learnt that he should not say, *'Surely not, Lord!'* when God said that something was fit to eat (Acts 10:14). What is more important is that God showed Peter that he should not say, *'Surely not, Lord!'* about the Gentiles receiving Christ and his Spirit. Gentiles and food were clean if God declared them so.

At first Samuel, Moses and Peter thought wrong. When they changed their minds and preconceived beliefs about themselves and God, they changed others. They finally got it right.

Change Your Mind

Some people say, 'I cannot do that', while others say 'I cannot change'. We should not allow weeks, months and years to go by without changing. We are encouraged not to conform to the pattern of this world, but to be transformed by the renewing of our minds (Romans 12:2). By refusing to change, we remain weak. Wrong thinking usually results in wrong feelings and consequently wrong actions.

> Progress is impossible without change; and those who cannot change their minds cannot change anything (George Bernard Shaw).

We must be willing to change if progress is to be made. Seven days without prayer makes one weak. The same is true of many things. Seven days without proper communication makes one weak. Seven days without speaking the truth makes one weak. Seven days without sex makes a marriage weak. Seven days without trusting God makes a Christian weak. Seven days without love makes a person weak.

Godly change and obedience to Christ turns weakness into strength. Time is short. We must be good stewards of our time. We can win through. Former heavyweight boxing champion of the world, Ray Leonard said:

> You have to know you can win
> You have to think you can win
> You have to feel you can win [1]

So let's be winners in our walk with Christ.

Chapter 21

Unique

When a visiting speaker came to our church one Sunday evening, it turned out to be very special. The praise that evening was especially exuberant. It was truly a celebration. Throughout the evening I was feeling expectant, that something would happen in my favour. I was praying that the preacher would prophesy the word of the Lord to me. I knew that this person had been used in this way before. It was almost as if I knew he would. I was full of hope.

When he finished speaking he pointed to four individuals in turn and spoke an encouraging, comforting and strengthening word to each. Gerald Coates spoke clearly, for all to hear. He then spoke to me, saying that in the future doors would be open for me to speak internationally. He said that God would use my charismatic personality and gifting. He said that there would be occasions when the gift of prophecy would flow through me.

People in church that evening were excited for us. I received the word as coming from God through one of his servants.

Something similar happened in the life of Nathanael:

> When Jesus saw Nathanael approaching, he said of him, 'Here is a true Israelite, in whom there is nothing false.'
> 'How do you know me?' Nathanael asked.
> Jesus answered, 'I saw you while you were still under the fig tree before Philip called you.'
> Then Nathanael declared 'Rabbi, you are the Son of God; you are the King of Israel.'
> Jesus said, 'You believe because I told you I saw you under the fig tree. You shall see greater things than that.'
> He then added, 'I tell you the truth, you shall see heaven open, and the angels of God ascending and descending on the Son of Man.' (John 1:47-51)

I received the word that Gerald had given. I weighed it up and believed it to be true. I kept it in my heart and waited for it to be fulfilled.

Three months later I attended the annual Evangelists Conference in Swanwick, England. During one meeting we got into small groups to pray together. Our group had just finished, others were still praying. A woman approached me and quietly said, 'I believe I have a word for you from the Lord. Can I tell you it?' At once I recognised her voice and knew her to be Jean Darnell. The essence of what she said was this:

> I see you with a microphone in one hand and a note book in the other. From your note book you are preaching other people's words and sermons. You are unique and original. Put the note book away. You are unique and original. Again I see you on a platform with your Bible in one hand and a microphone in the other. You are speaking powerfully God's word with the Bible to thousands. You are unique and original. Be so.

Somehow, by the gift of the Holy Spirit given to her, Jean Darnell knew something of my past, what I was like and predicted something about my future. Concerning the future - it came true. It was also true that I had been using other preachers' sermons. The emphasis on being unique and original was helpful and challenging for my formation. The part about speaking to large crowds with only my Bible and a microphone was to be fulfilled sooner than I knew.

A few weeks past. Korky Davey, a wonderful evangelist, invited me to be part of his team on a trip to Nigeria.

Of all places, why Nigeria? This was the most amazing and challenging time of my life. On the first Sunday of our trip, we were seated with the other leaders at the front of the church. There were thousands of people in front of us. Korky turned quietly and informed me that I was to speak. I was not prepared. Many thoughts rushed through my mind. My little sermon outline book was with me. I spoke to the best of my ability but I felt hindered, not liberated. I was not entirely happy.

Why? I was tied down to notes. I had not learnt to be myself - unique and original as Jean Darnell had said.

For the first few days I took the little sermon outline book with me, but it did not help. The word given to me by Jean Darnell was for now and it came to mind vividly. I made the decision to leave behind the outline book; it was time to be original and unique, to depend on God and myself.

Each time I was asked to preach I spoke with only my Bible in hand. I spoke with passion from my heart. This was a new beginning for me. There would be more trips to Nigeria and visits to Cyprus, Ethiopia, France, Greece and Poland. On every occasion I would speak with the Bible in hand. I had learnt a valuable lesson; God has made me unique and original. There is no need to try and be someone else. The text-book definition of preaching is: 'God speaking through personality.'

You too are unique. There is only one of you. There is no one like you. You are unequalled. You are one of a kind. You were born an original. You are original - novel, inventive, and uniquely creative.

Say to yourself with humility:

> I am God's unique and original gift to my family, my friends, my church and the world.

We seem to be able to believe that God loves us but not believe that God likes us. But God does like us - so let's accept it and begin to like ourselves!

Chapter 22

Vision

Men and women are driven by hopes, dreams and visions of what might be.

In the dictionary the word vision is defined as the act or faculty of seeing or a thing or idea perceived vividly in the imagination. Vision is perception, understanding, imagination, foresight, insight, perspective, dreaming, and planning. A godly vision is a supernatural apparition that is, something seen with the help of God that is not physically there.

What is Vision?

Vision is not always easy to describe. Not everyone has vision, although all of us do have hopes and desires for ourselves and those close to us.

Moses was given a vision from God. The vision was to take the Israelites out of slavery into a land flowing with milk and honey. It was to be a place of their own, a country of freedom, where their children could grow up without suffering abuse. The new promised land was the vision Moses received while he was looking after Jethro's flock of sheep (Exodus 3:7-11).

The angel of the Lord appeared to Moses in flames of fire that came from a bush that was not burning. Moses stepped forward to investigate this strange sight. When Moses reached the burning bush God told him not to come close; Moses was standing on holy ground. God said:

I am the God of Abraham, Isaac and Jacob.

God had a job for Moses to do. Moses knew that the task would be difficult. It took forty years for the people of Israel to occupy their new land of freedom and provision. Moses did not occupy the land. The vision given to Moses was for the benefit of others. Vision is often for the benefit of others. Vision is cost-ly, as it was for Moses.

The apostle Paul was given a vision; to preach the good news of Jesus far and wide. Paul's vision consumed his life. Paul wanted all people to know the living Jesus. Paul's vision was for the benefit of others. The visions given to Moses and Paul governed their lives. Phil Grant describes what happens when vision is dominant in your life:

> A vision is the dominant factor that governs your life. It determines all the choices you are making. It's what's left after all the layers are peeled away like an onion. Clinging like glue to the inside of your ribcage. It's what your mind gravitates towards when it is not legitimately concentrating on something else. It's what determines your friendships and relationships that you are cultivating. It's what your prayers are about - what you dream about and are giving money toward. [1]

What Do Visions Look Like?

Visions face the future. A godly vision has concern for the future. If we do not plan for the future, we plan for nothing. Many think only of today, with little or no thought for their future, or the future of others. Visions take into account the world. This kind of vision fills a responsibility to do something for another person, group, or country. Martin Luther King Jr had a dream. On August 28th 1963 at the Lincoln Memorial, Washington, before television cameras, he declared his vision - 'I have a dream'. Here is part of it:

> ' ... I have a dream that one day on the red hills of Georgia, sons of former slaves and sons of former slave-owners will be able to sit down together at the table of brotherhood.
>
> I have a dream that one day, even the state of Mississippi, a state sweltering with the heat of injustice, sweltering with the heat of oppression, will be transformed into an oasis of freedom and justice.

I have a dream my four little children will one day live in a nation where they will not be judged by the colour of their skin but by the content of their character. I have a dream today!

I have a dream that one day, down in Alabama, with its vicious racists, with its governor having his lips dripping with the words of interposition and nullification, that one day, right there in Alabama, little black boys and black girls will be able to join hands with little white boys and white girls as sisters and brothers. I have a dream today!

I have a dream that one day every valley shall be exalted, every hill and mountain shall be made low, the rough places shall be made plain, and the crooked places shall be made straight and the glory of the Lord will be revealed and all flesh shall see it together.

... And when we allow freedom to ring, when we let it ring from every village and hamlet, from every state and city, we will be able to speed up that day when all God's children - black men and white men, Jews and Gentiles, Catholics and Protestants - will be able to join hands and to sing in the words of the old Negro spiritual, 'Free at last, free at last; thank God Almighty, we are free at last.' [2]

Visions often relate to a person. Nearly all the visions in the Bible come to an individual. In a similar way for a church or organisation the vision comes to the pastor or director - the recognised leader. Visions are clear. They are not vague. Visions are specific and can be talked about. When they are shared some people will want to be involved; some will pray, some will give financially.

God told Noah to build a boat in the middle of the desert, to hold hundreds of animals and some people. Noah did what God said although some people thought that Noah was crazy. He did an impossible but realistic task. God's visions are attainable. Visions are often bigger than your capacity or ability. Ralph Waldo Emerson said:

Unless you try to do something beyond what you have already mastered, you will never grow. [3]

Visions give energy. Thinking, hard work, and planning follows vision. Nothing great will ever be achieved with a lazy attitude for life. Energy will motivate others. When energy is used properly it will strengthen your faith and give you more strength. In finding your vision, you will find energy. Vision has much to do with the mind. We need to change the mind that is set. When Godly vision is followed, true values come into existence. When this happens boundless vitality is released.

Vision and the Consequences

A visionary takes risks. You cannot make changes without taking risks. Visions that are God ordained and followed through will succeed within time. Nothing is impossible with God. Visionary people will face difficulties; difficulties through lack of funds, opposition from Christians who do not agree with them, challenges from friends and family, temptation to doubt, and even struggle because maybe no one else will join you. An example is Jackie Pullinger who when turned down by a missionary organisation, went to Hong Kong by herself.

Do not be surprised at the necessity for change, for vision to be fulfilled, through the individual, church, or organisation.

Vision will face dissatisfaction when it is not fulfilled fast enough. Others may express dissatisfaction with the vision; they may agree with the mission statement but not with the way it is to be fulfilled.

Without Vision

Kings, queens, politicians, leaders, countries, governments, organisations, establishments, schools, individuals, everybody should have vision. Your vision may be to help someone else fulfil their vision.

Winifred Newman said:

> Vision is the world's most desperate need. There are no hopeless situations, only people who think hopelessly. [4]

When Joshua was about to lead the Israelites into the promised land he instructed three tribes, the Reubenites, the Gadites, and the half-tribe of Manasseh to help others possess the land before they could see their dream realised. The tribes were glad to obey Joshua's request.

> 'You are to help your brothers until the Lord gives them rest, as he has done for you, and until they too have taken possession of the land that the Lord your God is giving them. After that, you may go back and occupy your own land, which Moses the servant of the Lord gave you east of the Jordan towards sunrise.' (Joshua 1:14-15)

Rev. Samuel Folahan, the assembly pastor at Christ Apostolic Church in Ibadan, Nigeria, has served Dr S. K. Abiara, the senior pastor, for over twenty years. Samuel has seen to it that the vision of Dr Abiara is fulfilled. Samuel's first calling is to enable another's vision to be realised. Together they have seen incredible numerical growth. Their new church building, on the outskirts of Ibadan, holds over 40,000 people. Thousands have come to Christ. Many have been healed and delivered of evil spirits.

Without a vision there is trouble and sometimes disaster.

> *Where there is no vision the people perish* (Proverbs 29:18).

It is helpful to read this verse in different translations as it helps us to see the fullest meaning of the statement.

> *Where there is ignorance [lack of vision] people run wild* (Living Bible).

> *A nation without God's guidance [vision] is a nation without order* (Good News Bible).

History has surely shown this to be the case.

> *Where there is no revelation [vision] the people cannot restrain themselves* (New International Bible).

The verse continues:

> *...blessed or happy is the person who knows and keeps God's laws.*

Vision must come from God. Visions are prophetic.

When Samuel was a boy, visions were not common (1 Samuel 3). One night God spoke to Samuel as he was sleeping. Samuel responded by saying:

> *'Speak, for your servant is listening.'*

God revealed his plans to Samuel. Samuel was afraid to tell Eli what God had said in the vision, but he was faithful in declaring the vision and it came to pass.

> *The Lord was with Samuel as he grew up, and he let none of his words fall to the ground. And all Israel from Dan to Beersheba recognised that Samuel was attested as a prophet of the Lord. The Lord continued to appear at Shiloh, and there he revealed himself to Samuel through his word* (1 Samuel 3:19-21).

May the Lord trust us with his word and vision. He will, as we open ourselves to his spirit and remain humble, earnestly desiring that his will be done.

Finding Vision

How will your vision come? When will it come? Maybe through a letter or telephone call; while walking in the countryside; or in the shower; during a time of prayer or while reading the Bible; or maybe through a messenger God will give you a vision. You will know when it comes. It will be in his time, when you are ready, that he will speak. Be ready. Ask for it. Wait for it.

> *The vision awaits its time ... if it seems slow, wait for it, it will surely come, it will not delay* (Habakkuk 2:3).

Finding vision is not the same as receiving guidance. We can find vision through the scriptures.

> Two men look through the same bars:
> One sees the mud, and one sees the stars (Frederick Langbridge). [5]

When God called me into full time ministry he did so through a preacher and through scripture. I had an overwhelming desire to preach the gospel full-time. I had been an evangelist for many years, during my time as a student and in industry. My wife Annette and I attended a Christian conference. One evening Floyd McClung was preaching, and I felt the Lord speaking to me through him. When we returned to our chalet I shared my desire to be a full-time evangelist. I would give up my career as an engineer and the opportunities to move on and up that particular ladder of life. Annette agreed that this was the time to step out into a new life of ministry. She encouraged and supported me to do what I felt God was saying to me.

I shared with our friend and pastor, Tony, the way we were feeling. He encouraged me to get confirmation from the scriptures, before making any final decision. I am thankful for his wise counsel, for I have known those who thought God had spoken to them when he had not, the result was trouble.

For six months I prayed for confirmation and finally was confident to go ahead.

> *For God works in you both to will and to do his good pleasure* (Philippians 2:13).

God worked in me to desire to serve him in a full-time capacity. I knew that I was gifted to do the work of an evangelist. My experience confirmed this. Tony gave me opportunities for nearly two years to preach regularly in our church. A revelation or vision from the Lord to go into full-time ministry was connected to my gifting as an evangelist. An important aspect of finding vision is in realising that vision is in someway connected with our gifts. Our gifts and skills help us to determine what our individual vision should be. We can build and find vision. It comes through scripture, prayer, dreams, experience, and other people. Vision comes from God.

Visions rarely become a reality without the help of others. We need one another. We need to learn to stand together and sometimes to own another's vision. Peter Brierley has written one of the best books on vision. He says:

> One man or one woman may have vision but its fulfilment requires a church, a company, a battalion, all the work force, an army, a multitude to make it happen. Don't think yours is any different. If its worth accomplishing, it has to be accomplished through others. [6]

Vision must be followed through for it to succeed; determination is necessary. Benjamin Disraeli once said: 'The secret of success is constancy of purpose'. [7] Commitment produces results.

A vision must excite the imagination; without this it is likely to fail. Vision will stretch our faith and mind. Vision costs, in terms of money and time. Vision involves sacrifice; there is no gain without pain.

When Jesus is our vision we also have visions of our own for the benefit of others.

> Be thou my vision, O Lord of my heart,
> Be all else but nought to me, save that thou art;
> Be thou my best thought in the day and the night
> Both waking and sleeping, thy presence my light.
>
> Be thou my wisdom, be thou my true word,
> Be thou ever with me, and I with thee, Lord;
> Be thou my great Father, and I thy true son;
> Be thou in me dwelling, and I with thee one.

Be thou my breastplate, my sword for the fight;
Be thou my whole armour, be thou my true might;
Be thou my soul's shelter, be thou my strong tower:
O raise thou me heavenward, great power of my power.

Riches I need not, nor man's empty praise:
Be thou mine inheritance now and always;
Be thou and thou only the first in my heart:
O Sovereign of heaven, my treasure thou art.

High King of heaven, thou heaven's bright sun,
O grant me its joys after victory is won;
Great heart of my own heart, whatever befall,
Still be thou my vision, O ruler of all.

By Mary Elizabeth Byrne & Eleanor Henrietta Hull.

Be a visionary as we herald the 21st Century!

Chapter 23

Woman who Touched Jesus' Garment

He Did Not Care What Others Thought

Jesus was at the lakeside where a large crowd had gathered around him (Mark 5:21-43). Jairus, a synagogue ruler, came to where Jesus was. When he saw Jesus he threw himself at his feet and started to plead earnestly:

> *'My little daughter is dying. Please come and put your hands on her so that she will be healed and live.'*

Jairus humbled himself. He was an important man and was regarded so by those around him. He was responsible for looking after the building and supervising the worship at the synagogue. When Jairus threw himself at Jesus pleading him to heal his daughter, he was casting aside his dignity.

He also threw aside his pride. He humbled himself at Jesus' feet and pleaded for help. For Jairus there was too much to lose. His concern was that his twelve-year-old beloved daughter would be healed. It was not the time to let anything stand in the way.

Jairus did not care what others thought of him. Neither did he care what others might do to him because of his association with Jesus. He knew that the Pharisees and some of the people who attended the synagogue were not keen on Jesus. Jairus wanted his daughter to be healed no matter what the cost. The large crowd that surrounded Jesus did not put him off. He pleaded earnestly. Jesus responded.

One of my favourite verses of scripture is here in this story. It tells me so much about my Jesus:

> *So Jesus went with him* (Mark 5:24).

The story gets more wonderful and interesting. While Jesus and Jairus, along with a large crowd, are making their way to the home of Jairus to visit his sick daughter, Jesus meets a woman. This woman had suffered for twelve years from bleeding. She had heard that Jesus was in town. She had learnt that Jesus healed. She thought to herself,

If I just touch His clothes, I will be healed.

The woman felt unable to ask Jesus for healing. Those around her believed she was unclean before God because of her sickness. She was despised and rejected by society.

Her thought 'If I just touch the hem of his garment,' was more than sufficient, as far as Jesus was concerned, to gain her healing. Jesus did not regard her as unclean because of her illness, as the Scribes would have regarded her.

As Jesus and Jairus walked with the crowd, the woman got close enough to touch Jesus' garment. The very moment that the woman touched his garment her bleeding stopped and she was freed from her suffering. Immediately Jesus felt power going out of him. He turned around and said:

'Who touched my clothes?'

The disciples did not know who had touched Jesus. They could not find the person responsible. Jesus refused to go any further until he knew who had touched him. He looked around until he found out who had touched him.

The woman decided to make herself known. She fell at his feet. She was trembling with fear. She told him her story. Jesus lovingly said to her:

'Daughter, your faith has healed you. Go in peace and be freed from your suffering.'

Jesus gave this poor woman complete salvation. She was healed physically from her illness and suffering. She was healed spiritually because she had peace. Jesus publicly commended her. He wanted all to hear and know that she was free. In other words Jesus told those around the woman to back off and leave her alone, now and always. The woman was well in body and spirit.

While Jesus was still speaking someone from Jairus' house, came bringing news:

> 'Your daughter is dead,' they said. 'Why bother the teacher any more?'

This is where they went wrong. This is why we sometimes go wrong. They thought of Jesus as just a teacher. But he is more than that.

Jesus ignored what they said. He said to Jairus:

> 'Don't be afraid, just believe.'

I am so glad that Jesus does ignore us sometimes. Jesus ignores nonsense. Circumstances that seem hopeless or impossible do not affect Christ. Jesus affects circumstances. Jesus does what is good and right, regardless of what people think or do. Jesus looked at Jairus and encouraged his faith - *"just believe"*.

Jesus took Peter, James and John and left the rest behind. When Jesus reached the home of the synagogue ruler, he saw the commotion and heard the crying and wailing. He went into the house and said:

> 'Why all this commotion and wailing? The child is not dead but asleep.' But they laughed at Him.

Jesus put them all out except for the child's mother and father and three of his disciples. He went into the place where the child lay. Jesus took her hand and spoke to her:

> 'Little girl, I say to you get up.'

At once she stood up and started to walk around. When this happened everyone was completely amazed.

A few years ago, while in Africa, I met a most humble, gracious and Christ-like pastor named Emmanuel. He had grey hair and was in his sixties. In his book *Better Christian Living*, he describes how the Lord used him to raise people from the dead. One of these people was a young child. He writes:

> The writer was preaching in an open air service when a woman brought her dead child to him for prayer; but the writer advised her to listen to the word of God which he was preaching and believe in the name of the Jesus. The woman who was impatiently waiting for the preacher to cut short the sermon and pray for her dead child was returning from the house of a native doctor when she heard the preaching about the power and life in Jesus Christ. As the preacher continued with the powerful sermon, a miracle was wrought and the child was brought back to life. This resulted in her conversion. This was in Ghana in a town called Kade.
>
>   One day the writer was called urgently to pray for a man who had just died. By the time the writer reached the man's house, he was dead and many people were weeping and someone was sitting behind the dead man with his neck stiffened and eyes closed. The writer drove all the people from the room leaving only the man's wife and two brothers and after closing the door prayed for a few minutes and called the dead man's name in the power of Jesus Christ. The dead man opened his eyes and after a second call he responded and the five of them came out of the room. There was great amazement and praising of the Lord. This was also in Ghana at Asamankese. [1]

In Mark 5 we have two wonderful stories rolled into one; that of the woman who touched Jesus' hem and of the little girl who was raised back to life. We see Jesus the compassionate saviour and healer.

Remember when Jairus pleaded earnestly for help. Jesus gladly went with Jairus. Remember he kept looking around until he found the woman - he was determined to complete the healing by publicly commending the woman, by saying to her:

'*Go in peace.*'

Jesus kept Jairus going when all was lost:

'*Don't be afraid, just believe.*'

Jesus will keep us going when all is lost. He can turn our losses into gains.

We can learn from Jairus the importance of pleading earnestly, casting aside anything that might get in the way - even righteous pride and righteous dignity.

The woman's embarrassing and horrid illness was a stigma. The woman thought that just by touching Jesus' garment she would be healed. The woman's thoughts were full of faith:

'*If I just touch His clothes, I will be healed.*'

Reach out and touch Jesus. Jesus stopped the whole crowd for one woman, and he will do the same for you!

Chapter 24
X-ray

Doctors are helped by the use of x-ray machines. These machines emit invisible electronic radiation of short wavelengths that pass through the human body. The x-ray pictures produced show bones, organs and any abnormalities. By taking an inside look at our bodies doctors are often able to offer a cure for disease.

God also takes a look at the condition of our hearts. God searches and sees our innermost being. Allowing God to x-ray and search our hearts, motives and desires can lead to significant change. Real change requires an inside look. God can and will reveal our true state if we ask him.

David prayed,

> 'Search me, O God, and know my heart;
> Test me and know my anxious thoughts.
> See if there is any offensive way in me,
> and lead me in the way everlasting.'
> (Psalm 139:23-24)

David is concerned to know the state of his heart. He asks God to show him. David is also concerned about his thoughts and asks God to test him. Are David's thoughts good, bad or ugly? David does not want to deceive himself. He wants to know the true condition of his heart. Sin in the heart is David's concern. This is exploratory surgery for sin.

David needed God's help. He did not know if there was any offensive way in his heart. That is why he prayed:

> 'See if there is any offensive way in me and lead me...'

David showed enormous spirituality and humility. He was open to what God would reveal to him.

It is too easy to assume that all is well with the condition of our hearts. I have not met anyone with a perfect heart. Have you? Sin in the heart must be uncovered, looked at and dealt with. An inside look that causes real change is unnerving and so it should be. The diagnosis of sin is not a pleasant experience. We tend to resist whenever we can, preferring to think we have come further than we have. We simply must get to the core of the matter. The kind of change that most delights our Lord will never occur if we deal only with sin in behaviour or obvious sin, neglecting the sin of the heart. Let us examine sin in behaviour and sin in the heart.

The Sin of Behaviour and the Sin of the Heart

Sin in behaviour is obvious. Premarital sex, cheating on your wife or husband, physical or sexual abuse, being racist, taking drugs, stealing, being dishonest, reading pornographic magazines, watching pornographic films, are just a few obvious sins. These sins involve an outward expression and are easily spotted. These matters are clear-cut. These obvious sins can easily be talked about and preached about. It is sin of behaviour that the Church has concentrated on. Countless books have been written on these issues. Christians have rightly been warned about such issues. In the mind of the Christian, when they think about sin, it is usually to do with the sin in behaviour.

If there is to be real change in our lives we must not only concentrate on sin in behaviour. We must look at the sin of the heart that is just as serious, if not more so.

Jesus warned the teachers of the law and the Pharisees, calling them hypocrites. Although they gave a tenth of their herbs, they had neglected the more important matters of God's law - justice, mercy and faithfulness. Jesus did not say that tithing was unnecessary or unimportant. But he did say that justice, mercy and faithfulness were more important. Jesus said to them:

> 'How terrible for you, teachers of the Law and Pharisees! You hypocrites! You give to God a tenth even of the seasoning herbs, such as mint, dill, and cumin, but you

> *neglect to obey the really important teachings of the Law,*
> *such as justice and mercy and honesty. These you should*
> *practise, without neglecting the others. Blind guides! You*
> *strain a fly out of your drink, but swallow a camel!'*
> (Matthew 23:23-24 Good News Bible)

On the outside the Pharisees and teachers of the law were respectable, good and clean. But on the inside their hearts were full of greed and self indulgence (Matthew 23:25-26). Jesus told them to first clean the inside and the outside will also be clean. Jesus was concerned with the state of people's hearts.

Exposing sin of the heart is no easy matter. When the areas of justice, mercy and faithfulness are thrown out or neglected it is sin of the heart. Sin of the heart is when we have sacrificed someone's feelings in order to build our own self-image. Often the result is that people are crushed underfoot. Sin of the heart is when we compromise an opportunity to love or do something, in order to stay safe. These sins are much more difficult to recognise. Even when we do recognise the offence, we do not always call it sin. Sin of the heart often goes unnoticed. The problem in the heart is far worse than many suppose.

Changing Our Hearts

God can help us change. He can change our heart. God changes our heart through his Spirit, his Word and his people. Allow the searching illuminating light of God in your life.

> Search me ... and know my heart ... see if their is any
> offensive way in me ... (Psalm 139:23-24)

The heart can be desperately wicked. We can easily fool ourselves that all is well, when it is not. Allowing God to search us is not as easy as it sounds. It can be difficult and painful to give Jesus free access to search our hearts. This is an uncomfortable process, but essential for growth.

The Holy Spirit convicts us of our sin (John 16:8). This searching does not take place in a moment. It is a continuous process throughout our lives. We must allow our souls to find rest before God. Life can be fast and busy. Our minds are often occupied with many things. Be still before God. It is vital to find time to be alone with God. The Holy Spirit can search us best when we are quiet and still. Walk with God. Talk with God. Sense him speaking to you. Feel the searching work of the Holy Spirit.

More things happen when God talks to us than at any other time. We have traditionally placed great emphasis on one aspect of prayer, that is when we talk to God. For us to advance with God, he must speak to us. Let him speak to you. Listen to him.

One of the things I like to do is to get in the car and go to my favourite quiet spot. There I spend a few hours with God. Often I find that during the first hour I am finding rest in my soul. During the next hour I read some scriptures and think deeply about them. The third hour I commune with God. It is in that kind of environment that the Spirit of God is able to search me.

The Word of God can also search our hearts. Allow the words and promises to touch your heart. We need to be real here. Apply the Word of God to your situation and allow your mind to be touched by the truth from the Bible. Let the Word do its work.

> *All scripture is God-breathed and is useful for teaching, rebuking, correcting and training in righteousness, so that the man of God may be thoroughly equipped for every good work* (2 Timothy 3:16-17).

The purpose of God's Word is clearly stated, '*that they may be thoroughly equipped*'. Whoever we are, wherever we live, God's Word is relevant. God's Word instructs and shows the way forward, the way to progress and succeed. Most importantly it shows us how to have good hearts.

God's Word speaks and changes our hearts when we allow it to. There is something in God's Word that is useful for every situation that we may face. Jesus spoke about murder, adultery, divorce, making promises, loving enemies, giving to the needy, prayer, treasures in heaven, being anxious, judging others, persevering in prayer and in life (Matthew 5,6,7).

It is one thing to know God's Word. But it is another thing to put it into action. It can be difficult to allow God to touch our hearts, especially if we suspect that we need rebuking or correction. I have known few people who have been joyful when God has rebuked or corrected them!

Another way our hearts can change is through God's people. Christians can try to wriggle out of a difficult situation. We try to avoid being rebuked or corrected, especially through another person. Growth sometimes requires discomfort. It may be through long term friendships or even a chance meeting with someone. As a result our lives are enriched and our hearts can be changed. We may find the situation changes for the better. God can change our hearts. Your heart can change whilst listening to a speaker, when having coffee with a friend, through reading, listening to a tape, or while watching a video. Change can occur through a counsellor. Change can occur through a planned event. It may come suddenly and unexpectedly. We should be open and relaxed.

But be warned: sometimes a well meaning person, even a leader, can do great damage by the advice or suggestion that they give. Damage can be done whether the advice is acted upon or not. Christians in leadership positions have a privileged responsibility to be good shepherds. I have known leaders cause destruction by their inappropriate actions and words, even though they sounded good and godly at the time. Words said to us, especially those words that give direction, must be tested. We should test them with God's Word and share them with trusted friends. Jesus said:

> 'But if anyone causes one of these little ones who believe in me to sin, it would be better for him to have a large millstone hung around his neck and to be drowned in the depths of the sea. Woe to the world because of the things that cause people to sin! Such things must come, but woe to the man through whom thy come!' (Matthew 18:6-7).

God changes our hearts. He helps us change by searching us through his Word and his people. He can and will change us only if we are willing for him to do so.

Don't stay content as you are, become fully the person God wants you to be.

Chapter 25

Your Story

They Believed Because of Her Story

Jesus, tired by the journey, sat down by a well in Sychar in Samaria (John 4:4-42). The time was about noon and it was hot. A Samaritan woman came to draw water. Jesus started a conversation by asking her to give him water. She was most surprised as Jewish people did not associate with Samaritans and so she refused. Jesus continued talking with her declaring that he had water of a special kind that he could give to her. She was intrigued. How could Jesus give her water, for he did not have a bucket with which he could draw?

Jesus added that this living water he could give would quench her thirst and she would never need to drink again. She asked for this water. Jesus told her to go and bring back her husband. *'I do not have a husband'* she replied. Jesus said to her:

> *'You are right when you say you have no husband. The fact is that you have had five husbands, and the man you now have is not your husband. What you have just said is quite true.'*

She recognised Jesus as a prophet and tells him so. As Jesus continued to speak with the Samaritan woman, his disciples arrived and were surprised that he was talking with a woman, especially a Samaritan. She left her jar and went back into the town saying:

> *'Come and see a man who told me everything I ever did. Could this be the Christ?'*

They came out of the town and made their way towards Jesus to see for themselves. Many Samaritans from the town believed in Jesus because of the woman's story. They encouraged Jesus to stay with them. Jesus did so for two days.

> *And because of his words many more became believers.*
> *They said to the woman, 'We no longer believe just because*
> *of what you said; now we have heard for ourselves and we*
> *know that this man really is the Saviour of the world.'*

The Samaritan woman's story and actions caused many to believe and meet the Saviour of the world.

My Story - The Camp that Changed My Life

My friend, Kevin Lambert, invited me to join him at a Summer Camp for young people. He assured me that it would be most enjoyable. There would be plenty of time to pursue sport and other activities during the seven days there. To my mind the only down side was that it was a Christian camp; this meant that each morning and evening for over an hour there would be a Christian meeting with songs, prayer and a talk. I was not impressed by that aspect of the camp, but I told myself that I would put up with it and enjoy myself for the rest of the time.

I was in for a pleasant surprise. Kevin's brother David, drove us from London, to a little village in Surrey. About 140 teenagers, from far and wide, gathered for a week of activities. One of the things that impressed me was, that those who called themselves Christians, had something extraordinary, something different, something special. These young people had a living faith in Jesus Christ. I noticed it when they prayed. I noticed when they spoke to each other about their faith. You could see it in their eyes and faces. It seemed to me that their Christianity was one of friendship with Jesus.

The other thing that struck me forcibly was the good news of Jesus that was presented. For three days I heard the old, old story. The story about Jesus of Nazareth, who came and lived in our world. He came and did good in a broken and needy world. I heard again the stories from the gospels. They suddenly became relevant and challenging.

I was told about the Son of God who died a horrid death by crucifixion. He died because I needed forgiveness and a new start. Believing seemed to take on another dimension with a greater understanding, involving the heart and mind. These words came to me strongly:

> 'Here I am! I stand at the door and knock. If anyone hears my voice and opens the door. I will come in and eat with him, and he with me' (Revelation 3:20).

I interpreted Christ's words as an invitation to me, with a promise on his part. With my heart I believed that the moment I invited Christ to come into my life he would do so, it was a certainty. It was automatic - if I asked, he would come. Jesus was waiting, knocking gently. It was a decision for me to make. Would I open the door and let Jesus in or not?

That was in July 1973, in a little village in England, one evening at 10.00 p.m., when I opened the door. It was a moment of repentance, and acceptance of Jesus Christ. I had read the Gospel booklet. It reminded me that God so loved the world that he gave his only Son, so that I might have life.

I opened the door and said these words:

> Lord Jesus Christ, I know I have sinned in my thoughts, words and actions. There are so many good things I have not done. There are so many sinful things that I have done. I am sorry for my sins and turn from everything I know to be wrong. You gave your life on the cross for me. Gratefully I give my life back to you. Now I ask you to come into my life. Come in as my Saviour to cleanse me. Come in as my Lord to control me. Come in as my Friend to be with me and I will serve you all the remaining days of my life, in complete obedience. Amen. [1]

I had begun the journey into life. The difference in me was immediate. During those first days and weeks my life and attitude changed. Jesus had become real. Prayer was like speaking with a friend. It was the day that changed my life. The result would affect my life, career, whom I married, how I acted and how I thought. Everything seemed to change. Being a Christian was wonderful; there was peace within, peace with God and peace with myself. I began to experience a different and greater purpose for my life.

My reasons for responding to Christ were twofold. Suddenly I believed that Christianity was true. That being the case there was only one thing I could do, embrace it. Not only was it true but I could see that Christ and Christianity were relevant to me and to life. C. S. Lewis, the Cambridge University professor and author, wrote:

> Christianity is a statement that if true is infinitely important, if false of no importance, but one thing it cannot be is moderately important.

For me that day the claims and life of Christ mattered enormously. It seemed to me that because Christianity was true, that only a positive response was possible. However, God has given us a freewill and He leaves it to us to decide what to do with him.

The other reason for responding to Christ was that I realised that I was not a Christian. This fact shocked me. Being baptised, attending church each week, praying and believing, does not make a person a Christian. I had thought that these things qualified me. I discovered that a real Christian was someone who knows Christ personally. Someone who communicates with God as opposed to someone saying prayers. It was the day that changed my life.

Your Story

Every Christian has a story to tell. Paul the apostle told his story to King Agrippa (Acts 26:4-24). Paul divided his story or testimony into three sections. He described his life before his conversion. He lived as a Pharisee, obeying strict rules. He opposed the Christians, sending them to prison. Many times he went from one synagogue to another to have Christians punished. Paul admitted to having had an obsession of persecuting Christians in the cities he visited.

In Paul's second section in Acts 26:12-18, he tells of his conversion. He was on his way to Damascus, with the authority and the commission of the chief priests, to persecute more Christians. It was about noon when suddenly a light, brighter than the sun, blazed around Paul and his companions.

> 'All of us fell to the ground, and I heard a voice say to me in Hebrew, "Saul, Saul! Why are you persecuting me? You are hurting yourself by hitting back, like an ox kicking against its owner's stick".
>
> 'Who are you, Lord?' I asked.
>
> And the Lord answered, "I am Jesus, whom you persecute. But get up and stand on your feet. I have appeared to you to appoint you as my servant. You are to tell others what you have seen of me today and what I will show you in the future. I will rescue you from the people of Israel and from the Gentiles to whom I will send you. You are to open their eyes and turn them from darkness to light and from the power of Satan to God, so that through their faith in me they will have their sins forgiven and receive their place among God's chosen people".'
>
> (Acts 26:14-18 Good News Bible)

When Paul had finished speaking about his dramatic experience he told his listeners what has happened since his conversion. He has been obedient to the words and vision, going first to Damascus, Jerusalem, the region of Judea and to the Gentiles, preaching the death and resurrection of Jesus and the forgiveness of sins.

Sharing our story is telling others what the Lord has done for us. We are new creations, the old has gone and the new has come. It is sharing something of our real experience with the living God our Saviour. He is a God who is close and who answers when we call out to him. Our story is that of an experience with the risen Jesus. We are told that the Gospel of Jesus Christ is powerful, bringing people to salvation. Likewise our story, told in an appropriate way, led of the spirit, is powerful.

> *'They overcame him by the blood of the Lamb and the word of their testimony.'* (Revelation 12:10)

So tell your story.

Chapter 26
Zacchaeus

Zacchaeus was wealthy. He worked for the Roman Government as a chief tax collector. He was responsible for the collection of taxes throughout the region. Ordinary tax collectors worked under his authority.

In those days the Roman Empire placed heavy taxes on all the people under their control. The Jewish people were not in favour of taxes, as this went to support a secular government. However, payment was forced upon them. Jewish tax collectors, like Zacchaeus, chose to work for the Romans. He was considered by Jewish society as a traitor. At best he was disliked, at worst hated. He was rejected, an outcast and sinner. Zacchaeus used his position and office to his advantage by unlawfully extracting money to line his pocket.

One day Jesus was passing through Jericho (Luke 19:1-10). Zacchaeus wanted to see what Jesus looked like. Zacchaeus had no apparent needs. He had no need of physical healing. He had no question to ask Jesus. He had no request to make of Jesus. He did not need any money. All he wanted to do was to see Jesus.

Zacchaeus was a short person and could not see over the crowd, neither could he get through them. He ran ahead of Jesus and climbed a sycamore tree and waited.

When Jesus reached the tree, he looked up and asked Zacchaeus to come down for he wanted to spend the day at his home. It was a divine appointment. Zacchaeus came down immediately and welcomed Jesus gladly. The people saw all that happened and said disapprovingly:

He has gone to be the guest of a "sinner".

Jesus was well aware of the state of Zacchaeus' life. Jesus wanted to bring him salvation. Zacchaeus noticed what the people were saying and thinking. He stood up and shocked everyone except Jesus by saying,

> *'Look, Lord! Here and now I give half of my posses-*
> *sions to the poor, and if I have cheated anybody out of*
> *anything, I will pay back four times the amount.'*

It is almost unbelievable - half of his possessions to the poor.
Very few had been willing to do such a thing. No wonder Jesus
praised him highly.

> *Today salvation has come to this house, because this*
> *man, too, is a son of Abraham. For the Son of Man*
> *came to seek and save what was lost.*

Although the Jewish people excluded Zacchaeus, Jesus recognised him to be part of society with all its blessings. Jesus put
the record straight, effectively saying to Zacchaeus, 'You are
included in the blessings of God. Do not be concerned with
what they think.' As usual, Jesus did not mind what others
thought of what he said and did. He always did what was right.
Jesus was himself and the truth mattered to him.

Jesus The Incomparable

We have in this story an important summary of Jesus' purpose
- to bring salvation, eternal life and the Kingdom of God.
Salvation is very broad. Jesus came to seek and save humanity,
which is lost without him.

Zacchaeus changed his lifestyle from the day he met Jesus. He
would no longer cheat anyone. He repented - he changed his
mind, which affected his actions. Jesus brought salvation to
Zacchaeus - a better life in this world and life after death. Jesus
forgave him. He accepted Zacchaeus' offer to pay back any
money he had cheated from the people.

I have always liked this little man. He was curious and open to
Jesus. He overcame his shortcoming - his height. He overcame
the crowd. Jesus could only help Zacchaeus because Zacchaeus
helped himself. God helps those who help themselves.

Jesus came to seek and save what was lost. He saves all who
come to him. Christ is the great Saviour. He saves us from our

sins. He saves us for heaven. He saves us from mediocrity. He saves us from ourselves; for at times we are our own worst enemy. He saves us from harmful habits. He saves us from selfishness and hate. He brings love and joy into our lives. He gives us direction and purpose. He saves the rich and the poor. He saves people from all cultures, countries, and backgrounds. He saves men, women, and children. He saves the wise, and the ignorant. He provides and protects. Yes, he offers salvation, full and free.

We begin to experience Jesus' salvation when he saves us from our sins, but he goes beyond this and saves us for many things. He lives to save humanity.

The story is told of a lady missionary whose service in the Gospel led her to visit the tents of nomadic Arabs who passed, and camped near the town where she lived. On one of her visits, she came to a tent where a woman stood, engulfed in deep sorrow and anxiety. Entering, she saw lying on a mat on the floor, an Arab lad, sick. Emaciated and evidently dying of tuberculosis.

She asked the mother, 'May I tell him a story?' Receiving a nodded assent, she knelt down beside the lad and began to tell the story of our Lord and his sufferings and death for sinners. She described how he was beaten, crowned with thorns, led out of the city of Jerusalem, nailed to a cross and left to die. The lad lay with closed eyes, but towards the end of her narration, he opened them and appeared to take some interest in the story. She left, to return the next day, when she told the same story emphasising that the blood of Jesus Christ was shed on the cross for the forgiveness of the lad's sins if he would only come to Jesus. This time the sick boy showed a greater interest and his face seemed to lighten up toward the end of her narration.

Next day, thinking it might be well to introduce something new into her message, she began to tell of the birth of Christ and was describing the place where he was born when the sick lad raised his hand and said, 'Not that! Not that! Tell me about the cross and the blood and the forgiveness of sins.' And again the same moving story was told.

When the lady missionary returned again some days later, she found the woman still sad and weeping bitterly: but there was no lad on the mat inside the tent. She asked the mother how he had died. The mother, when she saw he was dying, had called the Mohammedan priest who came with the Koran and began to read aloud to the dying lad. Then she described how he had feebly raised his thin hand and said, 'Not that! Tell me about the cross and the blood and the forgiveness of sins.' [1]

Do you know him? Have you experienced his great salvation? How shall we escape if we neglect such a great salvation?

The Bible says my King is a seven way King:
He's the King of the Jews - that's a racial King.
He's the King of Israel - that's a national King.
He's the King of Righteousness.
He's the King of the Ages.
He's the King of Heaven.
He's the King of Glory.
He's the King of Kings and he's the Lord of Lords.
That's my King.
... Well, I wonder, do you know him?

David said, *'The heavens declare the glory of God and the firmament showeth his handiwork.'*
My King is a sovereign King - no means of measure can define his limitless love.
No farseeing telescope can bring in the visibility, the coastline of his shoreless supplies.
No barrier can hinder him from pouring out his blessings.
He's enduringly strong.
He's entirely sincere.
He's eternally steadfast.
He's immortally graceful.
He's imperially powerful.

He's impartially merciful.
.... Do you know him?
He's the greatest phenomenon
that has ever crossed the horizon of this world.
He's God's Son.
He's the sinner's Saviour.
He's the centrepiece of civilisation.
He's the only one qualified to be an all-sufficient Saviour.
... I wonder if you know him today?

He supplies strength for the weak.
He's available for the tempted and the tried.
He sympathises and he saves.
He strengthens and sustains.
He guards and he guides.
He heals the sick.
He cleanses the lepers.
He forgives the sinners.
He discharges debtors.
He delivers the captives.
He defends the feeble.
He blesses the young.
He serves the unfortunate.
He regards the aged.
He rewards the diligent and
He beautifies the meek.
... I wonder if you know him?

Well, this is my King.
He is the King!
He is the key to knowledge.
He's the wellspring of wisdom.
He's the doorway of deliverance.
He's the pathway of peace.
He's the roadway of righteousness.
He's the highway of holiness.
He's the gateway of glory.
... Do you know him?

Well, his office is manifold.
His promise is sure.
His life is matchless.
His goodness is limitless.
His mercy is everlasting.
His love never changes.
His word is enough.
His grace is sufficient.
His reign is righteous and
His yoke is easy and
His burden is light.

I wish I could describe him to you.
But he's indescribable.
He's incomprehensible.
He's invincible.
He's irresistible!

Well, you can't get him out of your mind.
You can't get him off of your hand.
You can't outlive him and
You can't live without Him.
Well, the Pharisees couldn't stand him,
but they found out they couldn't stop him.
Pilate couldn't find any fault in him.
The witnesses couldn't get their testimonies to agree.
Herod couldn't kill him.
Death couldn't handle him and
The grave couldn't hold him.
That's my King! [2]

Sources of Help

National Society for the Prevention of Cruelty to Children
Child Protection Helpline *Tel. 0800 800 500*

Local NSPCC offices can be found in the local telephone directory.

Childline
Tel. 0800 1111
or write to:
Freepost 1111
London NI 0BR

Childline (Scotland)
Tel. 0141 552 1123

National Children's Home
85 Highbury Park Road
London N5 1UD
Tel. 0171 226 2033

(The NCH has eleven treatment centres in the UK for abused children.)

Childwatch
206 Hessle Road
Hull, North Humberside HU3 3BH
Tel. 01482 25552

For Survivors:

Most **Rape Crisis Centres** now offer counselling for women survivors of child sexual abuse. Local Rape Crisis Centres are listed in the telephone directory. Among the largest are:

London Rape Crisis Line
P.O. Box 69
London WC1X 9NJ
Tel. 0171 837 1600

Manchester Rape Crisis
P.O. Box 336
Manchester M60 2BS
Tel. 0161 834 8784

Leeds Rape Crisis
P.O. Box 27
Leeds LS2 7EG
Tel. 01532 440058

Liverpool Rape Crisis
P.O. Box 64
Liverpool L69 8AP
Tel. 0151 727 7599

Edinburgh Rape Crisis
P.O. Box 120, Head P.O.,
Brunswick Road
Edinburgh EH1 3ND
Tel. 0131 556 9437

Bangor Rape Crisis Line
Abbey Road Centre, Bangor
Gwynedd LL57 2EA
Tel. 01428 354885

Belfast Rape Crisis Centre
P.O. Box 46
Belfast BT2 7AR
Tel. 01232 249696

Other helping resources include:

Rape and Sexual Abuse Support Centre
P.O. Box 908
London SE25 5EL
Tel. 0181 688 0332

Shanti
1a Dalbury House
Edmondbury Court
Ferndale Road
London SW9 8AP
Tel. 0171 733 8581

Incest and Sexual Abuse Support
85 Millgate
Newark on Trent
Notts. NG24 4UA
Tel. 01636 610313

Women's Therapy Centre
6 Manor Gardens
London N7 6LA
Tel. 0171 263 6200

Women and Medical Practice
40 Turnpike Lane
London N8 0PS
Tel. 0181 888 2782

Christian Survivors of Sexual Abuse
c/o St John the Baptist Church
3 King Edward's Road
Hackney
London E9

Safety Net
c/o St George's hospital
Tooting
London SW17

For Black and Ethnic Minority Women:

Southall Black Sisters
52 Norwood Road
Southall
Middlesex
Tel. 0181 571 9595

Muslim Women's Helpline
Tel. 0171 700 2507/2509

Lambeth Women and Children Health Project
407 Wandsworth Road
London SW8 2JQ
Tel. 0171 737 7151

Young Asian Women's Project
6-9 Manor Gardens
London N7 6LA
Tel. 0171 272 4231

Subah
P.O. Box 30
JEDO Manchester M12 4LL

For Men:

Survivors
P.O. Box 2470
London W2 1NW
Tel. 0171 833 3737

Post-Survivors Group for Men
c/o Fighting Back
P.O. Box 1968
London N8 7AW

**Project for men who have been
sexually abused**
Off Centre
25 Hackney Grove
London E8
Tel. 0181 986 4016

**MOVE (Men Overcoming
Violence)**
c/o Friends Meeting House
6 Mount Street
Manchester M1
Tel. 0161 226 1216

For Survivors of Ritual Abuse:

Beacon Foundation
3 Grosvenor Avenue
Rhyll
Clwyd LL18 4HA
Tel. 01745 343600

SAFE
23 Highfield Road
Amesbury
Wiltshire SP4 7HX
Tel. 01980 623137

For People With Learning Difficulties Who Have Been Sexually Abused:

RESPOND
c/o 89 Ashurst Drive
Barkingside, Ilford
Essex 1G6 1EW
Tel. 01483 418075

For Deaf People Who Have Been Sexually Abused:

**Keep Deaf Children Safe
Nuffield Hearing and Speech
Centre**
325 Gray's Inn Road
London WC1X 0DA Tel.
Margaret Kennedy
Tel. 0171 833 5627

For Mothers of Abused Children:

Mothers of Abused Children
25 Warnpool Street
Silloth, Cumbria
Tel. 016973 31432

**MOSAC (Mothers of Sexually
Abused Children)**
P.O. Box 1008
Edinburgh EH8 7TH

Shale (for Asian mothers)
Tel. 0161 225 5111/9293

Refuges and Housing For Young Women Escaping From Sexual Abuse:

CHOICES (Cambridge House for Incest Survivors)
7c Station Road
Cambridge CB1 2JB
Tel. 01223 314438/467897

1 in 4 Project
c/o Bradford Resource Centre
31 Manor Row
Bradford BD1 4PS
Tel. 01274 305276

Washington Women in Need
1st Floor, The Elms
Concord
Washington NE37 2BA
Tel. 0191 416 3550

For Abusers:

Everyman
30a Brixton Road
Kennington
London SW9 6BU
Tel. 0171 793 0155

Bibliography

Chapter 1: Abuse

1. *The Subtle Power of Spiritual Abuse*
By Johnson & VanVonderen
Bethany House Publishing

pages 20-21

2. *Walking out of Spiritual Abuse*
By Marc Dupont
Sovereign World International Books

pages 8-9

3. *Manipulation, Domination and Control*
From Friends, Family and in the Church
By Prince Yinka Oyekan Junior
New Wine Press

page 11

4. *The Subtle Power of Spiritual Abuse*
By Johnson & VanVonderen
Bethany House Publishing

page 32

5. *Walking out of Spiritual Abuse*
By Marc Dupont
Sovereign World International Books

page 34

6. *Walking out of Spiritual Abuse*
By Marc Dupont
Sovereign World International Books

chapter 9

7. *The Seven Laws of Christian Leadership*
By Dr D Hocking
Regal Books

page 207

8. *Walking out of Spiritual Abuse*
By Marc Dupont
Sovereign World International Books

page 131

9. *Walking out of Spiritual Abuse*
By Marc Dupont
Sovereign World International Books

page 137

10. *Walking out of Spiritual Abuse*
By Marc Dupont
Sovereign World International Books

pages 140-141

11. *Walking out of Spiritual Abuse*
By Marc Dupont
Sovereign World International Books

page 142

12. *Walking out of Spiritual Abuse*
By Marc Dupont
Sovereign World International Books

pages 143-144

13. *The Subtle Power of Spiritual Abuse*
By Johnson & VanVonderen
Bethany House Publishing
page 67

14. *The Subtle Power of Spiritual Abuse*
By Johnson & VanVonderen
Bethany House Publishing
page 68

Chapter 2: Bartimaeus

1. *African-American Wisdom
A Book of Quotations & Proverbs*
Running Press Book Publishers
page 71

2. *African-American Wisdom
A Book of Quotations & Proverbs*
Running Press Book Publishers
page 110

3. *Quotes & Anecdotes for Preachers & Teachers*
Compiled by Anthony P Castle
Kevin Mayhew Publishers
page 17

4. *African-American Wisdom
A Book of Quotations & Proverbs*
Running Press Book Publishers
page 82

Chapter 3: Cross of Christ

1. *The Daily Study Bible Revised Edition*
The Gospel of Mark
By William Barclay
The Saint Andrew Press
Edinburgh
pages 360, 361, 362

Chapter 4: Don't Get on the Roof

1. *Quotes & Anecdotes For Preachers & Teachers*
Compiled by Anthony P Castle
Kevin Mayhew Publishers
page 49

2. *Quotes & Anecdotes For Preachers & Teachers*
Compiled by Anthony P Castle
Kevin Mayhew Publishers
page 49

3. *Between Friends*
by Mary Pytches
Hodder & Stoughton
pages 85-86

4. *Between Friends*
by Mary Pytches
Hodder & Stoughton
pages 85-86

Chapter 5: Enthusiasm

1. *Quotes and Anecdotes for Preachers and Teachers*
Compiled by Anthony P. Castle
Kevin Mayhew Publishers

pages 33-34

2. *Say Yes to Your Potential*
by Skip Ross
Word Books

page 123

3. *Courage & Confidence*
by Norman Vincent Peale
Cedar

pages 122-123

Chapter 6: Faith

1. *1200 Notes, Quotes & Anecdotes*
By A Naismith
Marshall Pickering

page 68

Chapter 7: Gifts

1. *Quotes & Anecdotes for Preachers & Teachers*
Compiled by Anthony P Castle
Kevin Mayhew publishers

page 110

2. *Quotes & Anecdotes for Preachers & Teachers*
Compiled by Anthony P Castle
Kevin Mayhew publishers

page 110

3. *Quotes & Anecdotes for Preachers & Teachers*
Compiled by Anthony P Castle
Kevin Mayhew publishers

page 110

Chapter 8: Holy Spirit

1. *Quotes & Anecdotes for Preachers & Teachers*
Compiled by Anthony P Castle
Kevin Mayhew Publishers

page 415

2. *The Normal Christian Life*
By Watchman Nee
Kingsway

page 91

3. *The Normal Christian Life*
By Watchman Nee
Kingsway

page 92

4. *The Normal Christian Life*
By Watchman Nee
Kingsway

page 92

Chapter 11: Keys

1 . *Quotes, Notes & Anecdotes for Preachers & Teachers*
Compiled by Anthony P Castle
Kevin Mayhew Publishers

page 89-90

2. *Quotes, Notes & Anecdotes for Preachers & Teachers*
Compiled by Anthony P Castle
Kevin Mayhew Publishers

page 378

3. *Quotes, Notes & Anecdotes for Preachers & Teachers*
Compiled by Anthony P Castle
Kevin Mayhew Publishers

pages 379-380

Chapter 12: Love Is …

1. *Quotes & Anecdotes for Preachers & Teachers*
Compiled by Anthony P Castle
Kevin Mayhew Publishers

page 361

2. *Quotes, Notes & Anecdotes for Preachers & Teachers*
Compiled by Anthony P Castle
Kevin Mayhew Publishers

page 68

3. *Quotes, Notes & Anecdotes for Preachers & Teachers*
Compiled by Anthony P Castle
Kevin Mayhew Publishers

page 68

4. *Quotes, Notes & Anecdotes for Preachers & Teachers*
Compiled by Anthony P Castle
Kevin Mayhew Publishers

page 13

5. *1200 Notes, Quotes and Anecdotes*
by A Naismith
Marshall Pickering

page 172

Chapter 13: Marriage

1. *Love is a Decision*
By Gary Smalley with John Trent
Word Books

page 91

2. *Knowing God*
By J I Packer
Hodder & Stoughton

page 189

3. *Conflict: Friend or Foe?*
By Joyce Huggett
Kingsway

page 169

4. *Conflict: Friend or Foe?*
By Joyce Huggett
Kingsway

page 162

5. *Conflict: Friend or Foe?*
By Joyce Huggett
Kingsway

page 163

6. *Conflict: Friend or Foe?*
By Joyce Huggett
Kingsway

page 171

Chapter 16: Perseverance

1. *Long Walk to Freedom*
By Nelson Mandela
Abacus
Tribute by David Steel MP

2. *An Enemy Called Average*
By John Marsh
Kingsway

3. *Quotes & Anecdotes*
For Preachers & Teachers
Compiled by Anthony P Castle
Kevin Mayhew Publishers

page 15

4. *Courage and Confidence*
Edited by Norman Vincent Peale
Cedar

page 26

5. *Quotes & Anecdotes*
For Preachers & Teachers
Compiled by Anthony P Castle
Kevin Mayhew Publishers

page 15

6. *Connecting*
By Paul D Stanley & J Robert
Clinton
Navpress

page 224-229

Chapter 18: Relationships

1. *Connecting*
By Paul D Stanley & J Robert
Clinton
Navpress

page 33

2. *Mentoring*
By Bobb Biehl & Glen Urquhart
Masterplanning Group
International

page 12

3. *Mentoring*
By Bobb Biehl & Glen Urquhart
Masterplanning Group
International

page 3

4. *Mentoring*
By Bobb Biehl & Glen Urquhart
Masterplanning Group
International

page 6

5. *Connecting*
By Paul D Stanley & J Robert
Clinton
Navpress

page 48

6 . *Connecting*
By Paul D Stanley & J Robert
Clinton
Navpress

page 65

2. *I Have A Dream*
By Martin Luther King Jr
Edited by James M Washington
HarperSanFrancisco

pages 104-106

3. *Leadership Summer 1994*
Volume XV Number 3
Subject - Vision

page 25

4. *Leadership Summer 1994*
Volume XV Number 3
Subject - Vision

page 25

5. *Leadership Summer 1994*
Volume XV Number 3
Subject - Vision

page 25

6. *Vision Building*
By Peter Brierley
Hodder & Stoughton

page 167

7. *Vision Building*
By Peter Brierley
Hodder & Stoughton

page 131

Chapter 23: Woman who
Touched Jesus'
Garment

1. *Better Christian Living*
by Rev Emmanuel L Asamoah
Fred Gay Printers (Nigeria)

page 26-27

Chapter 25: Your Story

1. *Prayer from Journey into Life*
By Norman Warren
Kingsway

Chapter 26: Zacchaeus

1. *1200 Notes, Quotes &
Anecdotes*
By A Naismith
Marshall Pickering

page 20

2. *Delivered live to an audience*
by Dr S F Lockeridge

The work and vision of Andy Economides is to preach the gospel and to see the Church renewed and revived.

Andy's passion is to spread the good news of Jesus Christ and to help others to reach out effectively in the UK, Africa and Europe. He trains leaders and churches in mission, evangelism and the nurture of new Christians. Since 1992, Andy has assisted Prospect College of Basic, Secretarial, Accounting and Computer Studies, Ibadan, Nigeria by raising funds, providing scholarships for poor students, providing typewriters and computers and helping to purchase land for the new college building. He serves Prospect College as its overseas director and is a member of Prospect's advisory board.

Andy originally qualified as a Mechanical and Production Engineer and worked for six years in research and development. From 1985-1995 he was on the staff of a church, working as an evangelist and Lay Minister. St. John's Theological College, Nottingham, awarded Andy Economides the College Hood in 1989 for completing a three-year course in Theological and Pastoral Studies. In 1994, Andy founded and is Director of Soteria Trust. He has ministered in Cyprus, Ethiopia, France, Greece, Nigeria, Poland and extensively in Great Britain.

The Soteria Trust Newsletter is available, free of charge, to anyone who is interested and who would like to be kept informed about the ministry. You may like to be involved financially and/or through prayer. The Partnership Project has been established to enable individuals or churches to be involved with the work. Soteria Trust would be happy to send you further information concerning the Partnership Project for your consideration, in which case please fill in the slip and send to the Soteria Trust office at the address below.

Like other charities, Soteria Trust relies on the generosity of people to support its work and to enable Andy Economides to preach the gospel in Great Britain and abroad. Like the Apostle Paul, Soteria Trust needs partners in the gospel.

'... *always pray with joy because of your partnership in the gospel from the first day until now.*' Philippians 1:4-5

For further information please send the slip to:

Soteria Trust
23 Windsor Road
Chichester
West Sussex   Tel. 01243 771494
PO19 2XF   Fax. 01243 771240

Registered Charity No. 1040766

--✂--------

○ Please send me the Soteria Trust Newsletter regularly

○ I would like to support the work of Soteria Trust and
   Andy Economides through prayer

○ Please send me further information about the
   Partnership Project

○ I enclose a gift of £_____ towards the ministry of Soteria
   Trust (please make cheques payable to 'Soteria Trust')

Name

Address

                              Postcode

Notes